LIFE LESSONS FROM MOM: FOR THE MAN YOU'LL BECOME

AMY TAN

AN AWARD-WINNING AUTHOR

Published in the United States by Books to Hook Publishing, LLC.

Edition: January 2025.

ISBN: 979-8-89283-209-0 (eBook)
ISBN: 979-8-89283-210-6 (Paperback)
ISBN: 979-8-89283-211-3 (Hardcover)

WINNER OF THE

LITERARY TITAN

GOLD BOOK AWARD

DECEMBER 2024

DEDICATION

To my son, whose thoughtful request for life lessons sparked the creation of this book. Your curiosity and desire to learn have inspired every lesson shared within these pages. Without your prompting, this book would never have been written.

Contents

Introduction

Son,

There are moments when every parent wishes they could hand their child a map—a guide to navigate the complexities of life.

You once asked if I had any wisdom to share—lessons that might help you navigate life's challenges. That question inspired me to compile this collection of insights—lessons I've learned, stories I've lived, wisdom I've gained, mistakes I've made, and triumphs I've celebrated.

Looking back, I stumbled at times because I didn't have the guidance I needed. What I'm about to share would have led me through moments of doubt, uncertainty, and challenge. But I've also learned that some lessons can't be taught—they must be experienced to be truly understood.

While these words are written for you, they are also meant for anyone seeking clarity, purpose, and direction in life. The lessons in these pages apply to all of us striving to live with intention, to love fully, and to leave a lasting legacy.

I share this with you, not because I have all the answers—far from it. If there's one thing I've discovered, it's that life is as much about the questions we ask as it is about the answers we find.

Life is a complex, unpredictable adventure. No book can provide all the answers, but I hope this one becomes your source of strength, a beacon of light, and a compass through the stories, struggles, and lessons that shaped my journey—so you too can walk your path with purpose, resilience, and strength.

Think of this book as my map for you—a thoughtfully crafted guide offering wisdom and practical insights.

It's a testament to my love for you and a reminder that you are never alone. As you navigate the ups and downs of life, remember that you can achieve great things, and I'm always here to support you.

1

Exploring Self: Beneath the Tip of the Iceberg

"Mastering others is strength; mastering yourself is true power."

—Lao Tzu

What if the only thing standing between you and a life of purpose is the person you see in the mirror? Before you can make your mark on the world, you have to understand what drives you, what fuels your passion, and who you really are. Without that deep self-awareness, you risk building someone else's dream instead of your own.

Think about it: How many times have you felt the tension between what you truly wanted and what others expected of you? How often have you let opportunities slip away because you weren't fully in touch with yourself?

If you're going to live a life that matters—a life people will remember—you need to start with the most important relationship you'll ever have: the one with yourself.

How Fear Blocked Me from $78 Million
A Costly Lesson on Self-Awareness

In 2011, just a few months after settling into our new home in Bangkok, I met Aaron, a fellow expatriate from New Zealand. He and his wife, an IT professional, were staying in the same serviced apartment as us while on a temporary work assignment.

One quiet morning after breakfast, Aaron approached me, his expression a mix of casual ease and something more urgent.

"Hey Amy, can I ask you something?" he began, skipping the small talk.

"Sure," I said, curious.

"I need to exchange some bitcoin for cash—200,000 baht, about $5,000. It's for my kid's school fees, and the regular channels will take too long. I could give you bitcoin for the cash. One bitcoin's worth $4.25 right now. What do you think?"

I blinked, the unfamiliar word catching me off guard. "Bitcoin?"

"Yeah," he explained, a spark of enthusiasm in his tone. "It's decentralized money—no banks, no government interference. It's the future, Amy. Trust me, this is big."

My gut tightened. The concept sounded vague, risky, even unreal. Using our hard-earned savings for something so intangible felt reckless. "I don't know," I replied slowly. "It sounds... uncertain."

Aaron leaned in, his voice earnest. "That's the point! This is cutting-edge. Imagine being part of something before the world even knows about it. Bitcoin could be worth millions someday."

Millions. The word echoed in my mind, but all I could see was the potential for loss. "I just... I don't think I can do it," I said, my voice firmer now, even though a small part of me was wondering.

He paused, disappointment flashing in his eyes. "Alright," he said softly. "But mark my words—you'll wish you had."

As he walked away, a small voice whispered inside me: What if he's right?

Today, bitcoin is worth over $67,000[1] per coin. That $5,000 would have grown into $78 million. Seventy-eight million dollars. I often think back to that morning in Bangkok, wondering how different my life might have been if I had simply said "yes."

But it wasn't just about the money. That decision revealed something deeper: my fear of the unknown, my reluctance to step into uncertainty, and how ignorance had built invisible walls around me. Fear, doubt, and cognitive bias—anchoring on what felt "safe" and familiar—kept me from seizing what could have been a life-changing opportunity.

I share this story because those same invisible barriers can keep us all from our true potential. The lessons from that moment have stayed with me: to question my assumptions, lean into discomfort, and open myself to possibilities—even when they seem risky.

What opportunities might you be letting slip by because of fear? Sometimes, the biggest risk isn't taking a chance—it's letting one pass you by.

Know Yourself

Knowing yourself—your values, beliefs, strengths, and weaknesses—lays the groundwork for wise decision-making, setting meaningful goals, and nurturing healthy relationships. Self-awareness serves as a compass, guiding you to face life's challenges with clarity and confidence, while ensuring your choices align with what truly matters to you.

Accepting and respecting your emotions is essential. In my younger years, I often ignored my feelings to gain acceptance, following the crowd despite a knot in my stomach. Each time I agreed to something that didn't resonate, I felt a hollow ache, as though I was betraying myself. Over time, I learned that suppressing my true self led only to inner conflict and dissatisfaction. Honoring your emotions and standing by your truth, even when it means standing alone, fosters a profound sense of wholeness.

Being true to yourself doesn't mean rejecting others or isolating yourself. Instead, it involves being honest about your feelings and making choices rooted in your values, rather than conforming to others' expectations.

Self-awareness isn't just essential for personal growth—it's also a critical component of professional growth. As highlighted by McKinsey's article *The 'Inside Out' Leadership Journey: How Personal Growth Creates the Path to Success*[2], the prerequisite for successful leadership in today's fast-paced, uncertain world is self-awareness and self-reflection. These abilities enable leaders to navigate complexity with clarity, resilience, and integrity.

By knowing yourself, you give yourself the gift of authenticity—a foundation for a meaningful, purposeful life. Embrace who you are, and let your inner value guide you through the journey.

Self-Reflection

Picture yourself at the edge of a calm lake, its surface so smooth it mirrors the sky, reflecting your own image back at you. But as you stare deeper, it's not just your face you see—it's the essence of who you are. There, just beneath the surface, lie your strengths, steady and clear, the traits that carry you through life's toughest moments. And yet, even in the stillness, small ripples appear—those inevitable moments of inner conflict that disturb the peace.

In the *The Road Less Traveled*[3], M. Scott Peck speaks of this kind of self-reflection, urging us to confront our inner selves with brutal honesty. Similarly, Carl Jung's philosophy emphasizes the importance of introspection. As he wisely said, *"Who looks outside, dreams; who looks inside, awakes*[4]*."*

Both Peck and Jung believed that true growth comes not from external validation, but from introspection—understanding the depths of your own mind and emotions. Their work on self-awareness highlights the importance of exploring your inner world, where you can confront fears, desires, and hidden truths.

Self-reflection isn't merely introspection—it's a transformative tool for personal growth. By confronting our inner selves, we foster deeper awareness and personal transformation.

So, as you reflect on yourself, what do you see? What are your greatest strengths? And when those ripples of doubt or uncertainty appear, how do you respond? It's in these moments of inner turbulence that we discover the clarity and courage to grow.

Observing Ego

Cultivating the "observing ego"—a psychological ability to objectively monitor our thoughts and behaviors—is crucial to this process. In *The Power of Now*[5], Eckhart Tolle highlights a similar approach he calls "witnessing presence," which encourages us to observe our mind and emotions as an impartial watcher.

By cultivating this observing stance, we create a buffer between our true self and the flow of thoughts, emotions, and actions. This space allows us to recognize patterns without becoming entangled in them.

This exercise of simply observing—helps dissolves automatic reactions and breaks the grip of ingrained habits, giving us the freedom to choose our responses consciously rather than react impulsively. This inner clarity not only deepens our self-understanding but also liberates us from the mind's habitual constraints, opening the door to emotional freedom.

However, even as we cultivate this mindful awareness, we must also acknowledge the impact of cognitive biases, which can distort perceptions and reinforce unconscious patterns. Cognitive biases often arise from past experiences and fears about the future, subtly influencing how we interpret present situations. As highlighted by the Cleveland Clinic article *Cognitive Bias 101: What It Is and How to Overcome It*[6], biases like confirmation, self-serving, attentional, anchoring, and actor-observer bias hinder objective self-assessment.

For instance, confirmation bias may lead us to favor information aligning with our beliefs while ignoring contradictory evidence. Similarly, attentional bias can narrow our focus, causing us to prioritize certain details while disregarding others.

Then there's anchoring bias, where the first piece of information we encounter often becomes the foundation for our judgment, skewing our perception from the start. Just like that morning in Bangkok, when I first viewed Aaron's bitcoin offer, I saw it through a lens of recklessness—a high-stakes gamble rather than an opportunity. That initial judgment anchored me in fear, shutting out the possibilities of what might have been a life-changing decision.

We all know the feeling: when things go right, self-serving bias tempts us to take full credit, yet when things go wrong, we're quick to point to external factors.

Actor-observer bias adds another layer, making it easy to spot the flaws in others while underestimating our own. These biases cloud our judgment, making self-reflection harder and growth more difficult.

I've had my own battles with confirmation bias at times, convincing myself that the evidence around me supported what I wanted to believe, even when deep down I knew it didn't. But what about you? How often do we let these hidden forces guide our decisions without even realizing it?

These moments of recognition, though uncomfortable, are where true self-awareness begins, helping us strip away the layers of bias that distort our judgment.

Facing Yourself with Compassion

Engaging in self-reflection can sometimes elicit distressing emotions, such as remorse or culpability for past behaviors, unrealized aspirations, or apprehension of failing. In these moments, practicing self-compassion is vital.

Mistakes are part of the journey. Acknowledge them, learn from them, but don't let them weigh you down. Give yourself the grace to move forward.

By engaging in self-reflection, you gain valuable insights into your actions and their impact on your life and those around you. Here's why it's essential:

- **Growth and Improvement**: Reflecting on your experiences helps identify areas where you need to grow. This continuous self-evaluation aids in becoming a better version of yourself, letting go of habits that no longer serve you, and developing qualities that support your aspirations.
- **Better Decision-Making**: Understanding your motivations enables you to make decisions that align with your values and long-term goals, rather than acting impulsively.

- **Emotional Regulation**: Reflecting on your emotions helps you understand why you feel a certain way and manage those feelings effectively, which is crucial for maintaining healthy relationships and managing stress.
- **Clarity and Focus**: Taking time to reflect clears mental clutter, bringing clarity and focus to what truly matters. It ensures your energy is focused on what aligns with your purpose and goals.

Embracing Your Strengths and Weaknesses

Personal growth requires acknowledging both your strengths and weaknesses. Here's how to approach this:

- **Recognize Your Strengths**: Take pride in your abilities and accomplishments. Your strengths are valuable tools for achieving your goals and overcoming challenges. Reflect on what you do well and how you can apply these skills in various areas of your life.
- **Accept Your Weaknesses**: Understand that everyone has areas for improvement. Accepting your weaknesses isn't about diminishing yourself, but about being honest and realistic. This self-awareness allows you to seek help when needed and develop strategies to grow.
- **Maintain a Balanced Perspective**: Both your strengths and weaknesses shape who you are. Embrace a balanced view that values progress over perfection. Celebrate your successes, and learn from your mistakes.

- **Commit to Continuous Learning**: Personal growth is an ongoing journey. Stay curious, seek feedback, and remain open to new experiences. Every step of growth brings you closer to your full potential.

By knowing yourself, practicing self-reflection, and accepting both your strengths and weaknesses, you pave the way for a fulfilling, purpose-driven life.

Dive into the Depths

A Journey Through Fear and Self-Awareness: Chronicled in the Revisiting the Depths: Overcoming Fear and Finding Peace[7]

One moment stands out in my journey to understanding myself—a moment when I had to confront not just external fear, but my deepest internal ones. It happened during a dive—one that forced me to face a trauma buried for three decades. As I stood on the boat, my chest tightened with anticipation. The surface of the water was calm—deceptively so—but beneath, I knew the depths held uncertainties I wasn't ready to face.

My breath came in shallow waves, fingers trembling as I gripped the edge of the boat. The weight of everything I had avoided for years felt heavier than the dive gear on my back. What if I'm not ready for this? With a deep breath, I slipped beneath the surface.

The cool water hit my skin, a sudden shock. Light from above quickly dimmed as I descended further into the depths. I felt the cold pressing in, and my thoughts raced, loud against the silence around me. What if I lose control down here? What if I can't come back up?

Each stroke pulled me deeper into the darkness, my grip on control slipping away. The deeper I went, the more I realized the ocean wasn't just a physical space—it mirrored the fears and emotions I had long kept submerged. Fear and uncertainty of the unknown clouded me. The currents tugged at me like thoughts I'd buried for too long. I wanted to resist, to turn back, but there was nothing to hold on to.

With my fists clenched, I struggled against the urge, but each motion served as a harsh reminder of the futility of control when faced with the unknown. I had to let go.

I realized the dive was never about controlling the waters or my fear—it's about trusting myself to navigate the unknown. In that surrender, I found clarity I'd been seeking all along. Just as the ocean demands respect and patience, self-awareness requires us to plunge beneath the surface of who we think we are, to confront the truths shaping our decisions.

After the dive, that sense of letting go shaped my life in ways I hadn't anticipated. The ocean taught me that, just as I trusted its unpredictability, I needed to trust myself amidst life's uncertainties. Surrender wasn't about giving up—it was about letting go of the need to control everything and allowing self-awareness to guide my actions.

Soon after, I faced a pivotal decision at work. Normally, I would have managed every detail, clinging to control out of fear. But this time, I remembered the dive. I remembered that clarity only comes when you let go. I stepped back, trusted my instincts, and let the situation unfold naturally. The outcome surprised me—it was better than I'd expected.

This shift extended to my relationships. I embraced vulnerability, trusting that honest, open connections would lead to stronger bonds. Letting go of control wasn't about weakness—it was about embracing trust in myself and others. These changes reflected how self-awareness helped me navigate fear and uncertainty—not through control, but through letting go.

What about you?

We all carry fears—some buried deep, others just beneath the surface. What are the fears that linger within you, and how might self-awareness help you release them? When you let go and trust yourself amid uncertainty, clarity often appears where you least expect it.

The journey into self-awareness is ongoing, much like the ocean—constantly shifting, always evolving. The deeper you dive, the more light you'll uncover, for even in the darkest depths, clarity and peace await those brave enough to explore.

So, what's keeping you from moving forward, and how can self-awareness guide you on your path?

Meaningful Insights:

- **Knowing Yourself**: Embrace your values, beliefs, and emotions without compromising your authenticity.
- **Self-Reflection as a Tool**: Regular self-reflection promotes growth, better decision-making, and emotional clarity.
- **Balancing Strengths and Weaknesses**: Recognize your abilities, accept your weaknesses, and remain committed to continuous learning.

2

Building Meaningful Connections

"A friend is someone who knows all about you and still loves you."
—Elbert Hubbard

Drown in the Digital Haze

It's a warm Friday evening, and my friends and I have gathered at our favorite rooftop restaurant, eager to reconnect after months apart. The air hums with laughter, the clinking of glasses, and the promise of stories waiting to be shared.

For a while, conversation flows effortlessly—talk of old memories, inside jokes, and the lives we've been living apart. But then, as if on cue, the devices come out. Jack is the first to glance down, thumb instinctively scrolling through Instagram on his iPhone, his attention slipping from the table. Across from him, Sarah snaps a quick photo of the appetizers, already crafting the perfect caption in her mind. Muthu, half-engaged, responds to a work email, his focus divided between the conversation and the glowing screen. I, although always the present one, sneak a glance at my WhatsApp, telling myself it's just a quick check for something important.

The energy shifts, subtle but undeniable. The conversation splinters into comments on memes and viral videos, punctuated by moments of silence as each of us drifts into our digital worlds.

"Remember when we used to hang out without these things?" Jack jokes, lifting his iPhone as if it were a foreign object, though he doesn't put it down. We chuckle, a fleeting moment of self-awareness, but the devices remain firmly in place.

I catch myself glancing up at the group, feeling a quiet tug of something I can't quite name. I watch Muthu's eyes dart between his screen and the conversation, and for a split second, I wonder if we've lost something we didn't even notice slipping away.

As the night wears on, the laughter continues, but something feels... thinner. There's a hollowness beneath the jokes and shared videos, a sense of missed connection that lingers in the air like a half-forgotten thought. The connection we used to have before social media carved out space between us.

When the bill comes, we all stand, hugging and promising to do it again soon. But as we walk away, I linger for a moment, my iPhone in hand. I scroll through the pictures from the evening and frown. Despite the laughter, despite the company, I feel a quiet emptiness I can't shake. It dawns on me that the night, once rich with the potential for genuine connection, had dissolved into moments passed through screens.

It wasn't just the night, I realize, but the depth of our friendships that had faded into the background, swallowed by the glow of our devices. How often do we truly take the time to nurture the friendships that mean the most to us?

I used to leave these nights with a warmth that carried me through the week. Now, the night has left me feeling disconnected, distant. If we don't start being truly present, I think, these friendships we hold dear might slip away entirely, unnoticed.

As I lie in bed, a quiet realization settles in: the relationships that matter most require more than a shared laugh or a digital comment. They need time, attention, and presence. Without it, they're at risk of fading, just like the memories of a night drowned in the digital haze.

Value of Friendship

The evening's disconnection made me think about the value of friendship, something discussed for centuries. Aristotle, an ancient Greek Philosopher, explored this theme in his work, *Nicomachean Ethics*[8], written around 350 BC.

Aristotle's definition of friendship encompassed many relationships, from family and friends to business partnerships.

He believed genuine friendship is built on virtue and mutual respect, not convenience or pleasure. The highest form of friendship, in his view, is one where individuals admire each other's character and genuinely seek each other's well-being.

These deep bonds, based on shared values and integrity, form the foundation of trust and loyalty. But such friendships are rare, requiring time and effort to cultivate—just like the connection I once enjoyed with my friends but felt slipping away that night at the rooftop restaurant.

In today's world, building meaningful relationships is increasingly challenging. While technology offers instant connections, it often comes at the expense of depth. Social media promotes fleeting interactions, leaving little room for lasting, genuine bonds.

Friendships can sometimes feel transactional—rooted in convenience or shared activities rather than the deeper, character-driven bonds that Aristotle believed were the essence of true friendship.

Yet, Aristotle's wisdom remains relevant. But how can we apply this ancient insight into our modern lives? Building lasting friendships takes more than just good intentions—it requires ongoing effort and mindful practices, such as deep listening, thoughtful communication, loyalty, trust, compassion, kindness, respect, support, and the ability to forgive.

By prioritizing these values, we can nurture relationships that go beyond surface-level interaction. Even in a busy, technology-driven world, seeking connections rooted in mutual respect and shared values allows us to experience the depth and trust that forms the foundation of genuine friendship.

Building Lasting Friendships
Practice Deep Listening

Deep listening is an art—one that invites us to set aside our own thoughts and emotions to truly focus on the other person. It's more than just hearing their words; it's about understanding the feelings, struggles, and experiences that lie beneath. We've all been there—trying to open up, being vulnerable, only to be interrupted by someone eager to share their own story or offer advice. It leaves us feeling unheard, as if our vulnerability was brushed aside.

I first learned about deep listening through an interview Oprah Winfrey conducted with Thích Nhất Hạnh[9], a renowned peace activist and prolific author. He described deep listening as a profound expression of love—offering the other person compassion that eases their pain. It creates a safe space where they feel truly heard and validated, especially when they're vulnerable. In that space, real healing and trust can take place.

So, the next time someone comes to you to talk, ask yourself: Am I really listening? In that moment, you have the chance to offer the gift of love, whether to share in their joy or ease their pain, deepening the bonds that connect us.

Thoughtful Communication

Open and honest communication is crucial for building a strong relationship. It's essential to share your thoughts, feelings, and concerns with those you care about. However, it's equally important to communicate thoughtfully, particularly in emotionally charged situations.

When we speak from a place of anger, our words can wound in ways that are difficult to mend. In those moments, it's wiser to pause—take a breath, collect your thoughts—before confronting the issue. By doing so, you can still express your feelings and concerns, but with a clarity that invites understanding rather than conflict.

Our words carry immense power—like swords that can either cut deeply or build bridges. In difficult situations, choosing your words with care ensures that your communication becomes a tool for connection rather than discord.

Show Respect, Support, and Forgive

Respect is the cornerstone of any healthy relationship. It means respecting your friends' and loved ones' opinions, boundaries, and individuality. Everyone has their own unique experiences, thoughts, and emotions, and part of valuing relationships is embracing these differences rather than criticizing or judging them. Accepting people for who they are, and celebrating their uniqueness, can lead to stronger, meaningful connections.

Being a source of support is just as important. Celebrating others' successes and standing by them during their struggles is a profound way to show you care.

I remember a time in my life when I was juggling the demands of motherhood, business, and personal growth. In the chaos, I sometimes neglected people who cared for me. Looking back, I wish I had made more time for them, especially when they were facing challenges. It's in those moments of support that friendships are truly fortified.

Forgiveness is another key element in relationships. No one is perfect, and misunderstandings and conflicts will happen. Holding onto grudges only poisons the relationship. Instead, practicing forgiveness allows both parties to move forward and grow from their experiences. When you forgive, you not only release yourself from the weight of resentment, but also open the door for healing and deeper connection.

Loyalty and Trust

Trust is built through a combination of consistency, honesty, and reliability. Keeping your promises, being transparent, and acting with integrity are the building blocks of trust. When you consistently show up as your authentic self, people begin to feel safe and comfortable around you. That sense of safety is crucial for fostering loyalty.

Think about a friend who always keeps their word; their reliability encourages you to lean on them during tough times, knowing they will not let you down.

Loyalty, though, goes beyond just sticking around. It's about building a bond that can withstand challenges and changes. It's about being there for someone through thick and thin, and knowing that they would do the same for you.

Being honest, even when it's difficult, is another cornerstone of trust. Sharing your true feelings and opinions, rather than hiding behind a facade, allows others to see your authentic self. This openness invites reciprocity, building deeper, more meaningful connections.

Reliability also plays a significant role. When you show up for others consistently, whether through a simple text to check in or helping with a project, people come to rely on you. Over time, this reliability becomes the foundation on which loyalty thrives.

Compassion and Kindness

Compassion and kindness lie at the very core of our humanity. Treating others with respect and empathy fosters an environment where everyone feels valued and supported.

Simple actions like listening to someone's troubles, offering a smile, or helping a friend in need can have a profound impact. These small acts of kindness ripple out, inspiring others to do the same. Imagine the power of one thoughtful gesture leading to a chain reaction of goodwill.

Think back to a time when someone extended compassion to you during a difficult period. How did it make you feel? Did their kindness bring you comfort or a sense of support you may not have realized you needed? Small actions can have lasting effects, and moments of compassion can strengthen relationships in unexpected ways.

Life is full of challenges, and when we respond to others with kindness during their hardest moments, we create a safe space for them to share their struggles. This not only offers them comfort, but also fosters a stronger bond between us. We all need that reminder that we are not alone in our struggles.

Choose Your Friends Wisely

The friends you choose have a significant influence on your life. Friendships shape who we are, affecting our thoughts, feelings, and actions. Supportive, positive friends can lift you up and inspire you to be your best self. In contrast, toxic friendships can drag you down, leading to negativity and self-doubt.

Choosing friends wisely means surrounding yourself with people who believe in you and encourage your growth. It's about seeking those who share your values and inspire you to become a better version of yourself. But it's equally important to recognize when a friendship is toxic. Ask yourself: Do I feel supported or drained after an interaction? Are my needs being met, or am I always giving more than I receive? Reflecting on these questions can help you recognize the relationships that nurture you and those that may hold you back.

Toxic friends drain you with constant negativity, jealousy, and a one-sided dynamic. They belittle your achievements, undermine your confidence, and leave you questioning your worth. In contrast, genuine friendships are a source of strength and joy—balanced, supportive, and uplifting. They celebrate your successes, lift you up in hard times, and encourage you to be your best self.

By being mindful of the company you keep, you give yourself the chance to cultivate relationships that bring out the best in you, while letting go of those that drain your energy and dim your spirit.

The Illusion of Connection

This truth became clear to me upon meeting Jenny. When she first walked into my office, her warm smile and the familiar aroma of my favorite coffee disarmed me instantly. She always seemed to know what I needed before I did, and at first, I welcomed her presence like a fresh breeze. But soon, our uninhibited laughter faded, replaced by silences that felt calculated, and every compliment she offered carried an edge—sharp, but almost invisible.

One afternoon, after yet another round of cutting remarks about our colleagues, I couldn't help but ask, "Why do you always have something negative to say about everyone?"

Her eyes locked with mine, her smile unwavering but cold. "I'm just telling the truth, Amy. You'll see soon enough."

It wasn't long before I noticed how every conversation revolved around her—her achievements, her struggles, her insights. Jenny would dominate the conversation, speaking at length while I listened, waiting for a chance to contribute. That moment rarely came. It had become a monologue. I realized that our relationship was not a two-way exchange, but a platform for her to perform.

It wasn't just the one-sided conversation. Jenny's manipulative tendencies surfaced in more troubling ways. She had an uncanny ability to create drama, spinning narratives that cast others in a negative light when they didn't align with her agenda. One by one, colleagues who didn't support her found themselves the target of her subtle but damaging character assassinations.

Her insecurities ran deep, though she concealed them well behind a façade of confidence. Jenny was swift to claim credit for successes, even when they were the product of teamwork. Yet, when things went wrong, she deflected blame and magnified others' mistakes to conceal her own.

Jenny thrived on control—of people, situations, and perceptions. Anyone who threatened that control became a target. Her charm was a mask, and beneath it lay a need for validation that could only be fed by diminishing others.

At first, I doubted myself. Could I be misreading her? Was she simply misunderstood? I even questioned my judgment, asking myself if I was overreacting. It's always easier to dismiss the warning signs, especially when doubt clouds your own instincts.

But when I finally sat in silence after yet another draining exchange, the truth became undeniable. I had become a tool for her validation.

I wasn't just observing her manipulation—I was experiencing it firsthand. Each interaction left me with a gnawing sense of exhaustion, as though I had been emptied without realizing it.

I finally understood that maintaining peace couldn't come at the expense of my own well-being. I had given too much of myself, and distancing myself wasn't just an option—it was a reclaiming of my power and my emotional energy.

Self-Reflection: Realizing the Harm

Looking back, I now recognize that Jenny exhibited many traits of what psychologists call a malignant narcissist[10]— someone who manipulates, dominates, and seeks to destroy in order to maintain control. At the time, I didn't have the words for it, but the emotional toll her behavior took on me was undeniable. It wasn't just her need for attention—it was the subtle, constant undermining of others to ensure she remained the focal point.

For months, I had been overlooking subtle signs, excusing her actions in the name of friendship. But now, the damage to my well-being—and even my reputation—was undeniable. I didn't confront Jenny directly—I protected my boundaries by quietly stepping back. Sometimes, stepping back isn't about confrontation; it's about preservation. It's about recognizing when a relationship is damaging to your well-being and having the courage to create space.

This clarity shifted my approach to relationships. I began seeking the reciprocity that Aristotle spoke of—where both friends strive for each other's good and mutual growth.

This shift helped me value friendships that brought joy and fulfillment while letting go of those that left me feeling depleted. Jenny's manipulative charm taught me a profound lesson: not every battle needs to be fought, but every boundary must be protected. By valuing myself and distancing from toxic relationships, I found the strength to nurture connections that bring joy and fulfillment.

A New Approach to Friendship

Toxic friendships, like the one I had with Jenny, often mask themselves as meaningful connections but, over time, drain your energy and self-worth. These relationships lack mutual respect, honesty, and the support that forms the foundation of healthy, loyal friendships.

Recognizing the signs of a toxic friendship is essential for protecting your well-being and ensuring that the people you surround yourself with are truly there for your growth and happiness.

Ultimately, the friendships you choose can lead to lifelong happiness or deep dissatisfaction. Cultivating positive, supportive friendships takes time and effort, but the rewards are worth it. With the right friends by your side, you can face any challenge that comes your way.

Meaningful Insights:

- **Value Friendship**: Genuine friendships provide love, support, and a sense of belonging, and they require consistent care and effort.
- **Cultivate Meaningful Relationships:** By practicing deep listening, thoughtful communication, respect, support, compassion, and kindness, especially during challenging times.
- **Choose Friends Wisely:** Surround yourself with friends who support your growth and let go of toxic friendships that drain your energy.

3

Growing Together: Navigating Relationships

"When we love, we always strive to become better than we are. When we strive to become better than we are, everything around us becomes better too."

—Paulo Coelho, The Alchemist

I Can't Help but Fall in Love with You

Imagine your eyes lock, and suddenly, the world fades away. In a room packed with people, it feels as though no one else exists—just the two of you. Your heart pounds in your chest, not from fear, but from a sensation so powerful it's almost overwhelming. Time seems to slow, each second stretching out as you become consumed in the moment.

Every word they speak feels charged with meaning, every gesture a secret language only the two of you can understand. The air between you hums with possibility, a spark that ignites something deep within. You feel weightless, as if gravity itself can't hold you down. It's both exhilarating and terrifying—an intense pull you can't resist, a leap you're ready to take without even thinking.

In that moment, nothing else matters. The world could spin out of control, but you wouldn't notice, because all that exists is the connection between you, real and electric, drawing you closer and closer.

That, my son, is the feeling of falling in love. It's magical, and for a while, everything seems perfect. You want to lock into this moment forever.

That's because falling in love triggers a powerful chemical reaction in your body. Dopamine, the "feel-good" hormone, floods your brain, creating feelings of euphoria. Norepinephrine makes your heart race, and oxytocin, the "love hormone," strengthens the bond between you and your partner, especially during moments of physical closeness[11].

But while these emotions and chemical reactions can make the beginning of a relationship feel magical, they're not the foundation for a lasting partnership. Building a meaningful bond requires continuous effort, patience, and understanding. As those initial feelings of excitement calm down, what remains is the connection you've created through respect, love, and kindness. That's when the real work begins.

As you continue to grow into the incredible young man I know you are, I want to share some thoughts with you about relationships—especially about how to treat a girl, whether she is your girlfriend now or your prospective wife in the future.

As you journey through life together, your partner will be one of your greatest allies, sharing in both your joys and challenges. While no relationship is without its ups and downs, embracing a few key principles will help you both cultivate a lasting, resilient partnership.

You might find it interesting to explore books like *Men Are from Mars, Women Are from Venus* by John Gray[12]. It offers some helpful perspective into the different ways men and women communicate and connect. While these insights are valuable, remember that individual differences are shaped by culture, experience, and personal history. So, the book is a guide, but the key to a successful relationship lies in understanding the unique person in front of you.

Stages of Relationship
Applying the Stages from *The Different Drum* by M. Scott Peck[13] to Relationships

One valuable concept from M. Scott Peck is the four stages of community—Pseudo-community, Chaos, Emptiness, and Community. Although these stages were originally developed to build strong communities, they are equally applicable to relationships. They help illustrate how connections move from surface-level harmony to deeper trust by navigating conflicts and embracing vulnerability.

Stage 1: Pseudo-community

In the early stages of a relationship, it's easy to present only your best self—avoiding conflict and maintaining a surface-level harmony. But genuine relationships thrive when both people can bring their full selves into the connection, flaws and all.

Application: Recognize that perfection is an illusion. Genuine relationships involve addressing differences and challenges.

Reflective Question: Have you noticed any moments in your relationships where you were avoiding conflict just to keep the peace? How might addressing these differences actually strengthen your bond?

Stage 2: Chaos

As you and your partner reveal more of your authentic selves, conflict is inevitable. The chaos stage is often where both people try to impose their expectations on one another, and things can feel unstable. But it's important to remember that this conflict is not a sign of failure—it's a natural step toward deeper understanding.

Application: Embrace conflict as a pathway to growth. It's natural and necessary, offering opportunities for deeper understanding.

Reflective Question: When conflicts arise, do you find yourself trying to impose your expectations on others? Can you approach these moments with more openness and understanding?

Stage 3: Emptiness

After the chaos, there comes a period of letting go—of releasing the need for control and shedding preconceived notions about who your partner should be. This stage of emptiness requires vulnerability, where you truly listen and open your heart to your partner without ego.

Application: Practice empathy, deep listening, and let go of ego. Building a genuine connection involves truly understanding and valuing your partner.

Reflective Question: Are there any preconceptions or expectations you might need to let go of in order to truly connect with your partner? How can embracing vulnerability help lead to a deeper relationship?

Stage 4: Community

Once you've worked through the conflicts and opened up to vulnerability, you reach a stage of true intimacy—the community stage. This is where trust and mutual respect flourish, creating a deep and meaningful connection where both people feel safe and appreciated.

Application: Foster trust and mutual respect. Celebrate each other's differences and create a space where both of you can thrive.

35

Reflective Question: What are some ways you can actively build trust and mutual respect in your relationship? How can you celebrate your differences while growing together?

By understanding these stages, you can appreciate that a meaningful relationship evolves through conflict, vulnerability, and, eventually, genuine connection. Encourage each other to grow as individuals while also strengthening your bond.

How to Treat a Girl: An A-Z Guide`

Below are some principles to help you navigate relationships with kindness, respect, and understanding:

- **Appreciate Her:** Show regular appreciation for who she is, not just how she looks. A simple "thank you" or acknowledging her efforts and achievements will make her feel valued.
- **Be Honest and Reliable:** We all make mistakes, but taking responsibility for them shows your character. She'll appreciate knowing she can count on you, whether it's through big promises or the little day-to-day moments.
- **Be Loyal and Trustworthy:** Loyalty is the cornerstone of trust. Be transparent, honest, and avoid

actions that might cause doubt. Consistency in your everyday actions will reinforce this trust.

- **Be Sensitive to Her Needs:** During certain times, like her period, she may need extra patience and care. Small gestures, such as offering her favorite snacks or just being present, can make a big difference.

- **Communication is Key:** Strong relationships are built on effective communication. Be open, honest, and willing to talk about everything, even the hard stuff. Listening is just as important as speaking.

- **Don't Talk About Your Ex:** It's usually best to avoid bringing up past relationships, especially in comparison to your current one. Talking about an ex can unintentionally hurt her feelings or make her feel less valued. Instead, focus on the unique connection you share with her.

- **Get to Know Her Beyond the Surface:** Take the time to really get to know her—the things she's passionate about, her dreams, even her worries. When you show genuine interest in who she is beneath the surface, it can deepen your connection in meaningful ways.

- **Handle Conflicts Maturely:** When conflicts come up—and they will—it's worth asking yourself if you're trying to push your own expectations too much. What if you approached these moments with a little more openness, a willingness to listen, and a desire to understand where she's coming from?

- **Kindness Goes a Long Way:** Small acts of kindness can go a long way. Thoughtful gestures, like writing her a note or helping her when she's stressed, can make a big difference.

- **Learn and Grow Together:** Think of your relationship as a shared journey where both of you are learning and growing. Embracing change together can bring you closer and help you navigate life's ups and downs as a team.

- **Love Unconditionally:** Embrace her fully, not as someone to mold or change, but as a unique individual with her own journey, strengths, and vulnerabilities. Accept her flaws and imperfections, and choose to love her every day.

- **Maintain Your Independence:** While it's wonderful to share your life with someone, don't forget to nurture your own interests and passions. Encouraging each other to pursue personal goals can make your relationship even richer and more fulfilling.

- **Navigating Dry Phases with Grace:** Every relationship hits a rough patch now and then. When that happens, try to be patient and keep the lines of communication open. Remember what brought you together in the first place and face the challenges together.

- **Practice Deep Listening and Empathy:** Really listening to each other can make a big difference. When you try to see things from her perspective and respond with kindness, it strengthens your connection on a deeper level.

- **Protect and Cherish Her:** Aim to build a space where she feels safe and appreciated. Valuing the time you share and being mindful of her well-being can deepen your relationship and make her feel truly cherished.

- **Provide Feedback Gently:** If you need to bring up something that's bothering you, try to do it gently. Using 'I' statements can help express your feelings without making her feel attacked. It's all about fostering understanding and working through things together.

- **Respect is the Foundation:** Take the time to understand her opinions, boundaries, and feelings—treating her with dignity will go a long way. It's easy to overlook the little things, but remember, respect is shown in the everyday moments.

- **Stay True to Your Values:** Always hold on to your core values like respect, kindness, and honesty. Let them be your compass as you navigate relationships—they'll help you build something healthy and loving.

- **Support Her Dreams:** It's important to support each other's dreams. When you encourage her to chase her ambitions and celebrate her successes, you show you believe in her. Be that person she can always turn to, whether the dream is big or small.

- **Treat Her Family with Kindness:** Getting to know her family can be a great way to deepen your connection. Showing genuine interest and respecting their values can help everyone feel more comfortable and connected.

- **Understand Her Triggers:** We all have things that set us off from time to time. Getting to know what triggers her will help you navigate tough moments with understanding and compassion. It's about being there for each other when things aren't perfect.

- **Observe What She Likes and Dislikes:** Pay attention to the little things—what she likes, what makes her smile. Knowing these details can help you create thoughtful surprises that show you really care, whether it's planning a special date or just a small gesture to brighten her day.

The Art of Growing Together

There's something beautiful about seeing someone evolve, knowing that you've been there for her journey. Growing together means being patient when things get tough, celebrating each other's victories, and being willing to change alongside one another. It's not just about building a life together; it's about building each other up, and that's where the magic of love truly lies.

But what if you find yourself attracted to someone else, even when you're in a relationship or already married? Son, if that ever happens, pause. Don't act on it. Attraction can feel intense, but it's a spark—a temporary rush that comes and goes. It's just a reaction in your brain, one that fades with time. Remember the chemical response we discussed earlier in this chapter. What matters more is the commitment you've made, the trust and loyalty you've built together.

Being faithful isn't just about resisting a momentary feeling; it's about choosing, day after day, to invest in the love and life you're creating with your partner. Don't let a passing feeling distract you from the connection and life you've chosen to build. True love isn't about the person who catches your eye in a fleeting moment; it's about the one who holds your heart through it all.

Now, if your partner betrays that trust—if she cheats— it's one of the most devastating experiences you may ever face. The pain of such betrayal cuts deeply, like a wound that seems impossible to heal. It's not just the act itself but the shattering of the bond you once held sacred, the doubts it sows about your worth, and the questions it raises about everything you've built together. In those moments, you'll feel hurt, angry, and disoriented, as if the ground beneath you has crumbled. It's a profound heartbreak that demands immense strength to navigate.

But here's what I want you to remember: betrayal doesn't define you. Sometimes, couples can rebuild trust and grow stronger from the experience, but it requires a lot of work, honesty, and both people being fully committed to healing. It's not easy, but it's possible.

That being said, reconciliation isn't always the right path. If trust has been broken beyond repair, or if the relationship becomes toxic, sometimes the healthiest option is to let go. Walking away in this situation doesn't mean you've failed. It means you're protecting your own well-being and making space for something healthier in the future.

Whether you choose to stay and work things out or walk away, know that healing takes time. You don't have to decide in the heat of the moment. Give yourself the grace to feel, to process, and to think about what's best for you in the long run.

What if you had kids? That adds another layer of complexity, and I want you to be mindful of that. In today's world, it's not uncommon to hear people talk about their stepfathers, stepmothers, and step siblings as if this is the new norm, a trend that's almost expected. But we can't ignore the emotional toll this can take on the children involved.

Kids often bear the weight of a separation. While adults may move on, children can struggle with the instability and confusion that comes with it. They may feel torn between parents, unsure of where their loyalty lies, or burdened by changes they didn't ask for. It's easy to talk about "moving on" or "blended families," but the emotional fallout for children can be long-lasting.

That's why, if you ever face this situation, consider how your choices will affect not only you but also your children. If there's a chance to rebuild trust and create a stable, loving environment for them, it's worth fighting for.

In the end, relationships are about resilience and intention. Challenges will arise, but how you navigate them defines your relationship. Let your choices be guided by respect and integrity, creating a foundation of strength and love that endures through every twist and turn of life.

Meaningful Insights:

- **Understanding the 4 Stages of Community to Build a Strong Relationship Foundation:** M. Scott Peck's four stages—Pseudo-community, Chaos, Emptiness, and Community—are essential to move through initial harmony, address conflicts, embrace vulnerability, and finally reach deep trust, creating a strong relationship foundation.

- **A-Z Guide to Relationships**: Appreciate your partner, communicate openly, respect one another, stay loyal, resolve conflicts maturely, support each other's growth, and cultivate a healthy interdependence.

- **Letting Go:** Sometimes letting go is the way to move forward. It's a step toward healing and growth, creating space for a relationship that aligns with your values and needs.

4

Into the Light: Grounding in Faith

"But the fruit of the Spirit is love, joy, peace, forbearance, kindness, goodness, faithfulness, gentleness and self-control."

—Galatians 5:22-23

We strive for success, but when the applause fades and the milestones are reached, what remains? For many, it's the search for something deeper—a sense of purpose that transcends material success.

Recently, the McKinsey Health Institute (MHI)[14] conducted a global survey of 41,000 individuals, revealing the universal importance of spiritual well-being regardless of age, country of origin, or religious affiliation. MHI defines spiritual health as encompassing more than just religious beliefs. It includes having a sense of purpose, meaning in life, and a connection to something greater than oneself.

This broader perspective on meaning is linked to stronger mental, social, and physical well-being. While this resonates with many, for me, spiritual growth is a journey deeply intertwined with my faith, guiding my every step. Though my faith has been central to my journey, others may find grounding in different beliefs, philosophies, or values.

Staying Grounded in Your Faith

As you journey through life, you'll encounter triumphs and joy, but also times of doubt, fear, and sorrow. And in those moments, it's easy to feel lost or overwhelmed. For me, staying grounded in my faith has been a vital anchor through life's ups and downs, offering a peace that transcends any earthly troubles. I'm reminded that the fruit of the Spirit is love, joy, peace, forbearance, kindness, goodness, faithfulness, gentleness and self-control. These are not mere ideals but the very essence of the Spirit we must welcome and embrace, shaping our lives with purpose and grace.

The Dark Side of Corporate Success

Faith was once my anchor, a steadfast foundation that guided my decision. It was the lens through which I viewed the world, shaping my values of integrity, compassion, and accountability. I believed my actions had purpose and that my work could serve a greater good.

Yet, there came a time when I strayed from that foundation. I'll never forget the turning point when I entered a leadership role in the corporate world. I often faced tough decisions—ones driven by the need to meet shareholders' interests and prioritize profit over ethics and long-term vision.

As the compromises became larger, I often wondered if I was complicit in the "corporate bodies of evil" that M. Scott Peck describes in *People of the Lie: The Hope for Healing Human Evil*[15]. In his book, Peck delves into the nature of human evil, including how it manifests in corporate and institutional settings.

He discusses how organizations can become "corporate bodies of evil" when they prioritize self-interest, deceit, and malice over ethical behavior and the well-being of individuals.

Living in such an environment, I felt a void. Despite some level of material success, a lingering emptiness haunted me. I thought that by relying solely on my own strength and wisdom, I could control my destiny and find happiness. But without a foundation to ground my choices, fear, pride, and selfishness often drove my decisions. And those decisions not only caused me inner turmoil but also had unintended consequences for the people around me—people I cared about deeply. At times, I betrayed the very values and beliefs I wanted to uphold, forcing me to confront the reality of who I was becoming.

Perhaps you've had similar experiences—moments when your values were tested, leaving you unsure of how to respond. Reflecting on these times can be invaluable. Being conscious of your values now will guide you to make decisions that align with who you truly are when life inevitably tests them.

Return to My Faith

During this period, everything seemed to be going well on the surface—my career was thriving, and I was hitting the milestones I had set for myself. But inside, I felt increasingly isolated and lost. Constant stress replaced any joy I once felt in my accomplishments. It was as if I were running on a treadmill, expending all my energy but never reaching contentment or peace.

The turning point came when the weight of my decisions became too much to bear. The pressure and emptiness overwhelmed me. In my desperation, I reached out to God, seeking His guidance and forgiveness. Returning to faith wasn't an instant fix; it was a gradual journey of healing and rediscovery.

These experiences became crucial points of self-reflection. It was only through reconnecting with my faith that I understood the true meaning of growth—not just outward achievements, but inner peace, resilience, and purpose. This process was painful, especially realizing how much I had erred. Embracing my faith again allowed me to make amends, face my weaknesses, and find the strength to move forward in a way that was true to both myself and those who care about me.

The Path of Redemption and Transformation

As I reconnected with my faith, I found that my approach to life and leadership transformed. Compassion, integrity, and sincere care for those around me became central to my leadership style. I believed we could achieve goals without compromising our values, despite pressures from shareholders. However, this approach had financial implications, and eventually, I found myself at odds with the company's direction.

When the COVID-19 pandemic struck in 2019[16], it brought unprecedented challenges—not only to the business world but to the way we lived and worked. The sudden shift to lockdowns, social distancing, and remote work disrupted supply chains and altered consumer behavior. For many companies, including ours, this resulted in a significant slowdown in sales and a sharp decline in cash flow. Fortunately, our company navigated the initial slowdown effectively, even growing because of our industry's resilience and strategic alliances.

But post-pandemic, the landscape changed. Retail sales declined, geopolitical tensions—especially Russia's invasion of Ukraine[17]—heightened, and economic instability followed. These combined factors created a perfect storm of challenges, forcing drastic measures within the company.

Ultimately, I had to leave, finding myself unable to align with the new direction. Perhaps this was God's way of saving me. Though painful, my departure allowed me to escape the moral conflict I felt, preserving my integrity and granting me peace.

Post-Departure Reflections

Post-departure was difficult, filled with uncertainties and emotional turmoil. Leaving the company after dedicating so much time and effort was agonizing. The achievements I had made felt overshadowed by the abrupt end, making the transition even harder to process. But leaving wasn't just a professional loss—it was deeply personal. The connections I nurtured and the strategic initiatives I led were integral to my identity. The abrupt transition forced me to reflect on both my successes and failures and find a path forward that honored my growth and align with my values.

Inspired by the principles of B Corporations[18], which advocate balancing purpose and profit, I found renewed purpose. B Corps prioritize the well-being of workers, customers, the community, and the environment. They strive to use business as a force for good, reducing inequality, lowering poverty, and building stronger communities. This resonated deeply with me, and I aspired to follow these principles. Companies registered as B Corps are living proof that this balance can be achieved. As responsible stewards of our organizations, we should strive to reach these standards.

Facing an unknown future, I clung to my faith, praying for guidance, trusting in God's plan, and finding solace knowing that He was with me every step of the way. This transition, though challenging, brought immense growth and strength. It taught me to rely more fully on God and seek His will above all else.

Reflections and New Beginnings

More than a year has passed since that eventful day when I realigned my professional life with my values. Now, I have the freedom to work alongside entrepreneurs who genuinely prioritize integrity, and a vision for long-term success beyond mere profit. This alignment has brought me professional satisfaction and personal peace. Additionally, my writing journey has brought profound fulfillment.

I realize I shouldn't aim to replicate my past role. Instead, I should open my heart to new endeavors. Only then will I truly embrace the path God has laid out for me—a plan to prosper me, not to harm me; a plan that protects my heart and soul; a plan that offers me peace that transcends all understanding.

Living a godly life is worthwhile. Building a relationship with God is paramount. It's a very personal and intimate journey, one of self-discovery and growth. And like any journey, it comes with moments of solitude and searching. But I have learned that even when we feel distant, remaining steadfast in our purpose and faith will ultimately lead us to the peace we seek.

Remember, son, a life lived close to God is a life well-lived. His presence will guide you. His love will sustain you, and His wisdom will illuminate your path.

Meaningful Insights:

- **Stay Rooted in Faith:** Faith provides the strength to navigate life's challenges with peace and purpose.
- **Success with Spiritual Values**: True success is aligned with spiritual values, not just material achievements.
- **The Power of Redemption:** Faith offers a path to healing and transformation, even after moments of crisis.

5

Integrity: The Anchor of a Meaningful Life

"Integrity is the seed for achievement. It is the principle that never fails."

—Earl Nightingale

When Integrity Meets its Rival

It was a typical Saturday morning, part of my usual routine to head to the Chong Nonsi station, the heart of Bangkok. The streets were alive, bustling with merchants, stalls of all kinds, and the scent of fresh food in the air. Tuk-tuks rattled by, their engines blending with the hum of voices. I bought my favorite fruits—grapes, apples, and pears—from a familiar vendor. But as I walked away, a flicker of unease crossed my mind. The lady may have mistakenly given me 5,000 baht ($150) in change instead of 500.

I stopped, the crumpled bills suddenly feeling heavier in my palm. A warm breeze brushed past, momentarily clearing my thoughts. Without hesitation, I turned around, my steps quickening as I retraced my path. The vendor's stall came into view, her face already turning to greet another customer. As I handed her the notes, her eyes widened in surprise—a flicker of disbelief crossed her features. She nodded, a small, grateful gesture, but her smile was what stayed with me. I walked away, feeling the warmth settle in my chest—not pride, but a quiet certainty. Integrity had been a reflex, not a decision, and it felt as natural as the bustling streets around me.

The most defining moments in life often happen in silence—when you make choices that no one else will ever know about. Integrity isn't always about grand gestures; sometimes, it's in the small, everyday decisions that shape who we are.

But what happens when the stakes are higher? When your integrity meets its toughest rival?

In the meeting room one afternoon, the air felt tense, heavy with unspoken pressure. The light buzz of the air conditioning was drowned out by the hushed conversations that fell silent as the meeting began. We had just received news that a team lead had committed an act of dishonesty, siphoning inventory merchandise for her own benefit. One of the management team leaned forward, his brow furrowed, his voice cold and final.

"We lump the total inventory losses onto Nurul," he said. "She broke the trust of the company."

My stomach tightened. I knew what they were asking was wrong, but in the corporate world, defiance often comes at a cost. Still, I couldn't remain silent.

"We can't do that," I argued, feeling the weight of every eye in the room turn toward me. "Yes, she may have stolen something, but that doesn't account for the entire variance in our inventory losses."

My role involved drafting the statutory declaration that would require Nurul's signature—essentially, it was a confession. But the sum we were attributing to her far exceeded what she had actually taken. The clean solution on paper was to turn the variance into a soft loan, something Nurul would pay off over five years. If she failed, she would live in constant fear of the company filing a police report.

The tension in the room was palpable, thick as a storm brewing just beneath the surface. It was a moment where integrity was pitted against power, and the stakes were far higher than the simple act of returning a few crumpled bills on a busy Bangkok street. Here, the consequences of compromising my values could ripple far beyond just myself—they could ruin a life for the sake of corporate convenience.

And then there was Mohammad.

"We will fire him," he said, his voice devoid of the admiration he once held for him. Just months ago, Mohammad had been hailed as a hero, praised for sealing a multi-million annual deal for the company. The management had celebrated him—he was the rising star, the man who had accomplished the impossible. But now, he was a target. His only crime? Speaking out, challenging the wrong people.

How could this be? One moment, Mohammad was celebrated, and the next, he was marked for removal. I watched as the corporate machine that once hailed his success now sought to discard him. Mohammad didn't understand the corridors of power, where quiet whispers and unseen influence held more sway than achievements. In the eyes of those in charge, he had crossed an invisible line.

I felt a wave of frustration and disbelief. These were the moments that truly tested your core. It's easy to do what's right when the stakes are low. But when your integrity clashes with power, and the stakes are high—that's when you find out what you're truly made of.

The Foundation of Character

Integrity and honesty aren't just ideals. They're the foundation of a meaningful life, shaping our every action, every decision, every interaction.

Think of integrity as the compass that points you toward true north, even when the path ahead is unclear. In the wilderness of everyday life—where distractions, temptations, and pressures abound—integrity ensures your choices align with your values, guiding you in the right direction when everything else pulls you off course.

Insights from Thought Leaders on Integrity

Integrity, as many thinkers have noted, forms the foundation of trust, and nowhere is this more evident than in the practice of honesty. As Earl Nightingale, a prominent motivational speaker and author, emphasized the crucial role of integrity in success with his famous quote, *"Integrity is the seed for achievement*[19] [20]*."* According to Nightingale, integrity wasn't just about honesty—it was the foundation upon which personal and professional success is built. He believed that living with integrity allows individuals to cultivate trust, credibility, and respect, all of which are essential for meaningful achievements.

Nightingale's perspective is echoed by authors like Stephen R. Covey in *The 7 Habits of Highly Effective People*[21], who described integrity as the glue that holds relationships together, both personal and professional.

Similarly, leadership expert John C. Maxwell in *Ethics 101: What Every Leader Needs to Know*[22] believes that integrity is a cornerstone of leadership, as it creates consistency between a leader's words and actions, ultimately inspiring confidence in others.

These thinkers suggest that while skills and talents are important, it is integrity that creates lasting success. Integrity ensures that achievements are built on a solid ethical foundation, allowing us to thrive in the long term.

Honesty: The Root of Trust

Honesty may not always offer immediate rewards, but it brings clarity, peace of mind, and reliability. When you are honest, others will know they can count on you. Your word becomes your bond. This trust will open doors for you in ways that dishonesty never could. More importantly, living truthfully brings peace of mind, knowing that you have stayed true to your principles, free from the burden of deception.

This peace, born from honesty, fosters a deep sense of self-respect and inner tranquility.

Staying True to Your Values

Life will tempt you with shortcuts and easier paths. It may sometimes seem simpler to lie to avoid trouble or bend the rules for a momentary gain. However, every time you compromise your values, you lose a piece of yourself. Staying true to your principles, even when it's challenging, shapes your character and becomes the hallmark of your moral strength.

Think back to the moments in your life when you felt a surge of pride—those rare instances when, despite the pressure to conform or take the easier route, you stood your ground. Maybe you lost something in that moment—perhaps the approval of others, an opportunity you desperately wanted, or even your sense of comfort.

What you gained was far more valuable: the quiet pride of knowing you stayed true to yourself. That pride, born from adversity, is the foundation of your strength and will carry you through life's toughest moments.

One of my favorite novels, *The Devil and Miss Prym*[23], written by Paulo Coelho, explores these very concepts. The story delves into the ethical dilemmas faced by a small village's inhabitants when a stranger tempts them with gold for committing a crime. Coelho's profound narrative addresses the nature of good and evil, the power of temptation, and the pivotal choices that define our moral compass. It explores the profound changes individuals undergo when faced with moral challenges and the transformative power of choosing the right path amidst uncertainty. Through this gripping tale, Coelho reminds us that the struggle between good and evil is a universal journey, and in facing these choices, we ultimately discover our true character.

Making Decisions with Integrity

There are moments when the choice to act with integrity feels like a sacrifice—perhaps it's choosing the truth even when it may lead to personal loss. These decisions are never easy, but they are the ones that define us.

In those moments, remember that integrity doesn't mean perfection—it means striving to be honest, genuine, and aligned with your values, even when it's hard.

The Stoic philosopher Marcus Aurelius, emperor of Rome from 161 to 180 AD, offered timeless advice on this in *The Meditations of Marcus Aurelius Antoninus*[24], a collection of his personal reflections written during his reign. He wrote, *"If it be not fitting, do it not, if it be not true, speak it not"*.

This simple yet profound statement captures the essence of Stoic belief: that integrity should guide every action, no matter the external pressures.

In moments when the right decision seems unclear, it's not just your values that guide you, but also your intuition. Your inner voice, often called a gut feeling, is shaped by your deepest values, experiences, and true self. It's also the voice of your conscience, reminding you of what truly matters and what aligns with your moral compass. It's the quiet whisper that can point you in the right direction when external pressures or distractions cloud your judgment.

In a world full of noise and competing expectations, tuning into your intuition requires moments of stillness. Whether through prayer, meditation, or simply a few minutes of quiet reflection, take time to listen to what surfaces in the silence. When faced with tough decisions, pause and listen to your gut instincts—are they aligned with your authentic self and core values?

The Ripple Effect of Integrity

Your choices, particularly those guided by integrity and honesty, will have far-reaching impacts on the world around you. Living with integrity inspires others to do the same, creating a ripple effect that extends beyond your immediate circle. In both your personal and professional life, your integrity can foster a culture of accountability, openness, and respect. Imagine how different the world would be if everyone made a conscious effort to act with honesty and integrity.

Practical Tips to Live with Integrity

Living with integrity is a daily practice. Here are a few practical ways to ensure your actions align with your values:

- **Pause Before Reacting:** When faced with a decision, especially under pressure, take a moment to reflect. Ask yourself if the action aligns with your core values.

- **Speak the Truth, Even When It's Hard:** Being honest, even in difficult situations, not only strengthens relationships but also frees you from the burden of deception.

- **Lead by Example:** Whether at work or in your personal life, demonstrate integrity through your actions. Others will follow your lead, creating a ripple effect.

- **Stay Consistent:** Practice consistency in the little choices, and they will shape your larger actions.

Living a Life of Integrity

Choosing to live with integrity and honesty isn't always the easiest path. It distinguishes you as a person of character and creates a journey marked by respect and inner peace. The benefits of living with integrity far outweigh any short-term gains that deceit or compromises might offer.

Consider the people you admire the most. I suspect many of them are individuals whose integrity and moral strength stand out. Their honesty likely influenced and inspired you, just as your choices will inspire others.

As you step forward into the unknown, hold these values close to your heart. Let your actions be anchored in integrity and allow honesty to be your constant companion.

With an open heart and integrity, you'll find the strength to live fully and inspire others. In those moments of challenge and uncertainty, remember that your actions leave an indelible mark on people around you. Through integrity, you will build a life that resonates with purpose, and you'll become the best version of yourself—one who stands tall, rooted in the values that matter most.

Meaningful Insights:

- **Integrity as a Core Value:** Integrity shapes your character, serving as a moral compass for everyday decisions and major life moments.
- **Living with Integrity**: Living with integrity means staying true to your values, acknowledging mistakes, and making amends, which fosters respect and builds character.
- **Impact of Integrity:** Acting with integrity inspires others, promoting a culture of trust in both personal and professional settings.

6

Facing Life's Challenges with Courage

---

*"The greatest glory in living lies not in never falling,
but in rising every time we fall."*

—Nelson Mandela

Face Challenges with Courage and Resilience

E very great story is shaped by moments of struggle—times when character is tested and resilience is forged. Resilience isn't merely the ability to endure hardship; it's the inner strength that propels us forward, even when the path is steep, pushing us beyond our limits and revealing strengths we never knew we possessed.

With every challenge, resilience teaches you to trust in your ability to overcome them. The greatest victories aren't achieved in the absence of struggle, but in the courage to face it, to rise again and again, no matter how many times you're knocked down. Each time you bounce back, you build layers of strength, preparing yourself for future challenges and triumphs.

Turning Mistakes into Growth Opportunities

Everyone makes mistakes; it's simply part of being human. However, mistakes can be powerful catalysts for growth. Think of a baby learning to walk—falling repeatedly but getting up each time stronger. Our missteps offer valuable lessons, helping us to refine our actions and understand ourselves better.

Approach your mistakes with curiosity, not shame. Ask, "What can I learn from this?" Treat yourself with kindness. Admitting mistakes is a sign of strength, showing honesty, humility, and a willingness to learn. It opens the door to growth and encourages others to embrace their imperfections as well.

When you realize you've made a mistake, take a deep breath and say, "I was wrong." It may be uncomfortable at first, but with practice, it becomes easier. The respect you gain from others—and from yourself—will be worth it.

Resilience in Action

In my early 20s, I had one all-consuming dream: to join a prestigious consulting firm with a global reach. I envisioned myself tackling complex business challenges for Fortune 500 companies and multinational corporations. Driven by this vision, I devoured books, improve my communication skills, and sought inspiration from those who had already achieved great success.

Finally, the moment arrived. I landed a position at a top firm, and the elation I felt was indescribable. It seemed I had reached the peak of my ambitions, filled with youthful idealism and ready to conquer any challenge. I dreamed of becoming a Partner in the firm someday.

But the glittering facade of my dream job quickly crumbled. What seemed like the perfect opportunity was filled with internal turmoil. My desk was situated directly in front of the Managing Partner, one of the most powerful figures in the firm. Initially, I saw it as a chance to learn from him, imagining the insights I could gain from his leadership.

However, my excitement soon gave way to disillusionment. The Managing Partner's volatile temper was a constant source of tension. I watched him hurl files, shout at colleagues, and berate managers and partners. His outbursts, visible to everyone through the office's glass walls, were unsettling. Instead of the inspiring mentor I had hoped for, I found myself trapped in a toxic environment where fear and anxiety were the norm.

There were days when I seriously considered walking away. The emotional strain was heavy, and the weight of constant anxiety was overwhelming. But deep down, something inside me refused to give up. I knew that if I allowed this situation to break me, it would define my future in ways I couldn't accept. So, I made a decision—to endure, to push through, and to find strength within myself, even when it felt like I had none left.

Resilience isn't just about bouncing back after a fall; it's about enduring in the moment, finding ways to keep moving forward when everything around you feels like it's crumbling. And that's what I did. I focused on what I could control, shifted my mindset from despair to growth, and reminded myself daily that this was just one chapter in my story, not the complete book.

That experience taught me that true resilience isn't forged in easy times—it's born in the fire of adversity. It's in those moments when you feel like giving up, but choose to keep going. In the end, it was that same resilience that led me to bigger opportunities, healthier environments, and a more fulfilling career and life.

Just as I discovered how resilience can shape personal and professional growth, others like Jeremy Camp and James Clear have used their struggles to inspire transformation. Their stories, like mine, serve as a reminder that adversity is not an end—it's a beginning, an opportunity for growth.

Inspiring Stories of Resilience
Jeremy Camp

One of the most heart-wrenching and inspiring stories in contemporary Christian music is that of Jeremy Camp[25]. His journey, marked by profound love, tragic loss, and unwavering faith, has deeply influenced his music and touched countless lives.

Camp's life took a significant turn when his first wife, Melissa, was diagnosed with ovarian cancer shortly after their engagement. Despite the devastating news, the couple chose to marry, reflecting their deep love and commitment. Tragically, Melissa passed away, just a few months into their marriage. This heartbreaking loss became a pivotal moment in Camp's life, deeply impacting his music and personal journey.

In the aftermath of Melissa's death, Camp was overwhelmed with grief, yet his faith remained steadfast. He found solace in writing music, channeling his pain into his art. In 2003, he released the song *I Still Believe,* a heartfelt anthem that expressed his enduring faith despite the heartbreak he had experienced.

His songs, like *I Still Believe* and *Walk by Faith*, offer comfort and encouragement, especially to those facing their own trials. What makes his music so impactful is its authenticity, born from real experience and genuine emotion.

Today, Camp continues to inspire millions, showing that faith and resilience can be powerful sources of strength in the darkest times. He reminds us that even in moments of profound loss, we too can rise, using our experiences to inspire and uplift others.

James Clear

Resilience applies not only to emotional hardship; physical challenges can also spark remarkable growth, as seen in the story of James Clear, the author of *Atomic Habits: An Easy & Proven Way to Build Good Habits & Break Bad Ones*[26]. Clear's journey began with a freak accident during his sophomore year of high school. While playing baseball, Clear was struck in the face by a bat, resulting in severe injuries. His recovery was long and challenging, involving multiple surgeries and a prolonged rehabilitation process.

The accident was a turning point for Clear—not just physically, but mentally. In *Atomic Habits*, he outlines how small, incremental changes can lead to significant improvements in life. Habits are like the compound interest of self-improvement, gradually building up. His principles—making habits obvious, attractive, easy, and satisfying—offer a practical guide to building good habits and breaking bad ones.

Clear's journey teaches us that resilience is not just about bouncing back from adversity but about using that adversity to build better habits and improve our lives one small step at a time.

Journeys of Faith, Habits, and Resilience

Both Camp and Clear have showed remarkable resilience in overcoming adversity. Camp's music and Clear's writings exemplify how faith, perseverance, and the pursuit of small, positive changes can lead to profound transformation.

Their stories remind us that life will inevitably present challenges and setbacks, but resilience allows us to turn those moments into opportunities for growth. Just as I learned through the disillusionment of my early career, you too can find strength and personal development in life's toughest moments by embracing them as stepping stones on your journey.

Believe in Your Journey

Life will throw its share of hardships your way, but it's how you respond to those moments that define your strength.

Resilience is not about being perfect; it's about being relentless in your pursuit of becoming a better version of yourself, even when the odds are against you. Embrace challenges; they strengthen you. Welcome mistakes; they teach valuable lessons. Trust your inner voice; it is the whisper of your conscience, guiding you towards your true path.

No matter how difficult the journey becomes, trust in your ability to adapt, grow, and rise above the obstacles.

Remember: You have everything you need inside you. Believe me, you possess more bravery than you realize, strength that surpasses what you appear, and intelligence beyond what you perceive. Trust yourself, believe in yourself, and keep moving forward one step at a time.

And don't forget to enjoy the ride. Life is more than reaching the finish line; it's about savoring the experience. Find joy in small moments, laugh often, love deeply, and live fully.

It is in your hands to craft the life you envision. It may not happen overnight, but with courage, resilience, and self-trust, you can make incredible things happen.

There is no greater adventure than pursuing the life you've always dreamt of living. The path won't be easy, but the outcome will always be worth it.

Meaningful Insights:

- **Challenges as Growth Opportunities**: Every challenge presents a chance for personal and professional growth, pushing us beyond our limits to become stronger and more resilient.
- **Embrace Mistakes with Curiosity**: Approach mistakes with curiosity, seeing them as valuable lessons that help refine actions and improve self-awareness.
- **Resilience in Adversity:** Resilience is about rising stronger after adversity, using challenges as a catalyst for transformation and personal success.

7

The Grace of Humility and Gratitude

"Gratitude is when memory is stored in the heart and not in the mind."

—Lionel Hampton

"True humility is not thinking less of yourself; it is thinking of yourself less."

—Rick Warren

H umility and gratitude aren't just fleeting moments of reflection; they are powerful tools that shape how we experience life. What if the secret to a happier life wasn't found in success or material wealth, but in something much simpler—humility and gratitude?

We all experience days when everything seems to go our way, and others when nothing feels right. Then, there are the in-between moments where life feels neutral and uneventful.

But no matter where we find ourselves, embracing humility and practicing gratitude can bring light to even the darkest times and add meaning to the most ordinary moments.

Humility

Humility isn't about thinking less of yourself; it's about knowing yourself—the good and the not-so-good parts—and accepting that there's always room to grow. Maybe you're great at solving problems or perhaps you're the person people turn to for support. These are your strengths, and it's important to recognize them, but remember: staying humble means not letting your strengths define your worth.

As Confucius wisely said, *"Humility is the solid foundation of all virtues[27]."* This highlights how humility serves as the cornerstone for all other virtues, anchoring us in self-awareness and motivating us to embrace lifelong learning and growth.

On the flip side, we all have weaknesses. Maybe public speaking terrifies you, or you struggle to stick to a morning routine. Rather than feeling defeated, see these weaknesses as opportunities for growth. Humility is about being real with yourself and others, embracing who you are without pretending to be something you're not. When you're humble, you don't need to show off or prove yourself to others—you can simply be yourself, and that's powerful.

Humility also shapes how we respond to external feedback. Mother Teresa captured this beautifully when she said, *"If you are humble, nothing will touch you, neither praise nor disgrace, because you know what you are[28]."* Her words reflect the idea that when we live with humility, we are not swayed by external validation—be it praise or criticism.

We all experience moments when praise lifts us up or criticism pulls us down, but humility allows us to stay balanced. By knowing and accepting ourselves, we learn that our true value comes from within, not from what others think of us. When you embrace humility, you stay steady through the highs and lows, finding fulfillment not in recognition, but in living authentically and purposefully.

Both Confucius and Mother Teresa remind us that humility is not only about understanding ourselves, but also about how we treat others. Mother Teresa's life was a testament to this, as she served others with humility, not seeking personal glory but finding joy in helping others.

Humility invites us to step back from our ego, listen to others, and continuously seek to improve, creating a life rooted in purpose, growth, and service to others.

Gratitude

Now, let's talk about being grateful. This is all about appreciating what you have in your life. It's so easy to focus on what we don't have or what we wish was different. But when we do that, we miss out on all the good stuff right in front of us.

According to psychologist Robert Emmons[29], one of the world's leading experts on gratitude, practicing gratitude has profound psychological benefits. His extensive research shows that gratitude not only improves mental health, fostering stronger relationships and enhancing life satisfaction, but it also increases resilience in the face of challenges. Grateful individuals tend to have a more positive outlook on life, finding strength and optimism even during difficult times.

Start small. Think about the basics—do you have food to eat? A roof over your head? Clothes to wear? These might seem like little things, but not everyone in the world has them. When you start to feel grateful for these basics, you'll see how much you really have.

Then, think about the people in your life. Your family, your friends, even the stranger who held the door open for you this morning. Each of these people adds something to your life. Maybe your dad always knows how to make you feel better when you're down. Or your best friend can make you laugh until your sides hurt. These are things to be grateful for.

Don't forget about experiences, too. Every day brings new ones, big and small. Maybe you saw a beautiful sunset, or you finally finished that book you've been reading. Perhaps you learned something new at school or work. Each of these experiences shapes who you are and adds color to your life.

Being grateful isn't always easy, especially when things are tough. But that's when it's most important. Even in hard times, there's usually something to be thankful for if we look hard enough.

When you're grateful, something magical happens. You start to see the world differently. Little things that used to bug you don't seem so important anymore. You feel happier and more content. And the best part? This feeling spreads to others around you.

Practical Tips for Staying Humble and Grateful

How do you stay humble and grateful every day? Here are some practical tips:

- **Start Your Day with Gratefulness:** Before you even get out of bed, think of three things you're grateful for. It could be something as simple as a good night's sleep or a warm cup of coffee. This sets a positive tone for your day.
- **Keep a Gratitude Journal:** At the end of each day, write down a few things you're thankful for. On tough days, look back at this journal to remind yourself of all the good in your life. It can be a powerful tool for maintaining perspective and positivity.
- **Say "Thank You" More Often:** Not just for big things, but for little things too. Thank the delivery driver, the cashier at the store, your coworker, your

friend, your partner, and your parents. Saying it out loud makes the feeling even stronger and helps build a culture of appreciation.

- **Help Others:** When you give your time or energy to help someone else, it reminds you of what you have to offer. It also enhances your gratitude for what you already possess. Volunteering or simply being there for a friend can make a big difference in both their lives and yours.

- **Learn Something New Every Day**: This keeps you humble by reminding you that there's always more to learn. It could be a new word, a fun fact, or a skill you've always wanted to try. Embrace curiosity and the joy of discovery.

- **Listen More Than You Speak**: Really pay attention when others are talking. Attempt to see things from their point of view, even if you don't agree. This fosters empathy and helps you learn from different perspectives.

- **Admit When You're Wrong**: It's not always easy, but it's a sure sign of humility. Plus, it shows others it's okay to make mistakes. Owning up to errors builds trust and demonstrates integrity.

- **Notice the Little Things:** The smell of fresh coffee, the sound of rain on the roof, the feeling of sun on your face. These small joys are everywhere if we pay attention. Mindfulness helps you appreciate the present moment and find beauty in everyday life.

- **Practice Self-Reflection:** Every now and then, take a good, honest look at yourself. What are you proud of? What could you improve? This helps you stay grounded and keeps your ego in check.

Staying Humble and Grateful—An Ongoing Journey

Remember, staying humble and grateful is an ongoing process, not an end goal. Some days, it will be easier than others. There will be times when you feel proud of yourself, and that's okay! What matters is staying grounded and not letting that pride overshadow your humility.

And there will be moments when gratitude feels elusive. That's okay too. On those days, be gentle with yourself. Sometimes, just being grateful for another day, another chance, is enough.

As you cultivate humility and gratitude, you'll likely notice shifts in your perspective and your relationships. You might find yourself more patient—with others and with yourself—and more at peace, even in imperfect circumstances.

You might also notice that your relationships improve. When you're humble and grateful, you're easier to be around. People are drawn to those who are genuine and appreciative.

The most profound change, however, might be in how you view the world. Instead of fixating on what's wrong or missing, you'll notice the abundance of good already present. This doesn't mean turning a blind eye to problems or pretending everything is flawless. It just means finding the balance between acknowledging challenges and appreciating blessings.

And here's a secret: the more you practice being humble and grateful, the easier it becomes. It's like exercising a muscle—the more you use it, the stronger it gets. Soon, it will start to feel natural, like a part of who you are.

So, as you go through your days, remember to keep your feet on the ground and your heart full of gratitude. Recognize your strengths, but don't let them make you feel superior. Acknowledge your weaknesses, but don't let them bring you down. Keep an open mind and be willing to learn from everyone and everything you encounter.

And always, always take time to appreciate the good in your life. From the biggest achievements to the smallest joys, there's so much to be grateful for. Let that gratitude fill you up and spill over into the world around you.

You have the power to choose how you see the world and how you move through it. By choosing humility and gratitude, you're not just making your own life better—you're making the world a little better, too. And that's something to be truly grateful for.

So, go ahead, take a deep breath, look around you, and say a quiet "thank you" for this moment, right here, right now.

You're alive, you're growing, and you have the chance to make a difference. Stay humble, stay grateful, and watch how it transforms your world.

It's a choice you can make every day. It's not always easy, but it's always worth it. And in the end, it leads to a richer, happier, and more meaningful life.

> **Meaningful Insights:**
>
> - **Humility Fosters Growth:** Embracing humility allows for personal growth, self-awareness, and the openness to learning from others, keeping arrogance at bay.
> - **Gratitude Shifts Perspective:** Practicing gratitude helps shift focus toward the positive, allowing for greater appreciation of both the small and significant joys in life.
> - **Strengthen Relationships through Humility and Gratitude:** Both qualities deepen relationships by fostering empathy, openness, and a positive ripple effect that inspires others.

8

Empowered by Positivity

"The more you praise and celebrate your life, the more there is in life to celebrate."

—Oprah Winfrey

L ife is like a roller coaster, full of highs and lows, but here's a secret: your attitude makes all the difference. When you choose positivity, you equip yourself with a powerful tool to face any challenge. Think of your mind as a garden—you can plant flowers or weeds. By approaching life with optimism, you're sowing the seeds of beautiful, vibrant growth. Each positive thought becomes a seed that blossoms into something wonderful.

The Power of Positive Thinking

There's a wealth of literature on positive thinking, highlighting its impact on our lives. From Norman Vincent

Peale's *The Power of Positive Thinking*[30] and Napoleon Hill's *Think and Grow Rich*[31] to Rhonda Byrne's *The Secret* [32]and Tony Robbins' *Awaken the Giant Within*[33], these books emphasize how a positive mindset can shape our reality. These authors provide invaluable insights on harnessing the power of positivity to transform our lives. Exploring these works can deepen your understanding of positive thinking and inspire you on your journey.

Practical Tips for Maintaining a Positive Attitude

- **Celebrate Others' Successes:** Be genuinely happy for the successes of those around you. This attitude fosters positivity and strengthens your relationships.
- **Cultivate Resilience:** Think of resilience as a muscle that strengthens with use. Each time you overcome a setback, you build resilience for future challenges.
- **Dance it Out:** Put on your favorite music and dance. Dancing is a fun way to lift your spirits and change your mood.
- **Embrace Change:** When you embrace change, you open yourself up to growth, adaptability, and a more optimistic view of the world.
- **Embrace Hope During Difficult Times:** Even when life feels overwhelming, remember that tough times are temporary. Think of challenges like storms—intense but

always passing. Hope is a guiding light that helps us see beyond our current struggles.

- **Embrace Positive Attitude:** No matter the situation, maintaining a positive attitude can profoundly affect your mood and outlook. Even when it feels challenging, choose positivity.

- **Find Beauty in Your Surroundings:** Take a moment to fully appreciate the natural beauty that is all around you. Whether it's the light streaming through the window or the colors of your environment, there is wonder everywhere if you take the time to notice.

- **Find Joy in Everyday Moments:** Life is made up of both big events and small, ordinary moments. The secret to happiness lies in finding joy in these everyday experiences.

- **Find Inspiration in Others' Stories:** Read about people who have overcome significant obstacles. Their resilience and courage can inspire and motivate you to face your own challenges.

- **Find Humor in Situations:** Look for the funny side of life's challenges. Finding humor can help you cope with difficulties and lighten your mood.

- **Find Your Tribe:** Build connections with like-minded individuals who share your interests and values. Surrounding yourself with such people brings mutual inspiration, support, and the chance to grow together in meaningful ways.

- **Find Lessons in Every Experience:** Seek the silver lining in every experience, even when times are tough.

- **Focus on What You Can Control:** *The Serenity Prayer*[34] reminds us to accept what we cannot change, have the courage to change what we can, and seek wisdom to know the difference. Focus your energy on areas where you can truly make an impact.

- **Keep a Positive Journal:** At the end of each day, jot down three positive things that happened. They don't need to be monumental—perhaps you shared a genuine laugh with a friend or felt a refreshing breeze on your face. By practicing this, you can develop the ability to redirect your mind towards positive thoughts.

- **Keep a Success Journal:** Document your achievements, big and small. Reviewing your successes can boost your confidence and remind you of your capabilities.

- **Laugh Often:** Laughter is a natural mood booster. It triggers the release of endorphins, which improves your mood and overall well-being[35]. Watch a funny movie, tell jokes, or be silly.

- **Limit Time with Negative People:** While you can't always avoid negativity, try to limit your interactions with negative individuals.

- **Nurture Your Passions:** Explore activities that not only bring you joy but also ignite a deep sense of fulfillment. Pursuing your passions adds meaning and satisfaction to your life.

- **Practice Self-Care:** Taking care of yourself physically supports mental positivity. Eat healthily, sleep well, and stay active. When you are in good physical condition, it becomes easier to maintain a positive outlook.

- **Practice Mindfulness:** Stay present in the moment to avoid worrying about the future or dwelling on the past. Mindfulness can help you find calm, even in chaotic times.

- **Practice Gratitude Daily:** Identify and appreciate three things you are grateful for each day. This practice shifts your focus from what's wrong to what's right in your life.

- **Practice Forgiveness:** Holding onto anger or resentment is burdensome. Forgive others and yourself to release negative energy and make room for more positive pursuits.

- **Practice Deep Breathing:** When feeling stressed, take a few deep breaths. This simple practice can calm your mind and help you regain focus.

- **Reframe Negative Thoughts:** Challenge negative thoughts and consider alternative perspectives. Often, our fears are not reflective of reality but of our anxieties.

- **Savor Your Experiences:** When you engage in activities, fully immerse yourself in the experience. Taste your food, embrace your loved ones, and breathe in the fresh air. By savoring these moments, you enhance your overall enjoyment of life.

- **Seek Support:** You don't have to face challenges alone. Reach out to friends, family, or professionals. Opening up about your challenges can bring a sense of relief and bring forth fresh insights.

- **See Problems as Chances to Grow:** Instead of asking, "Why me?" when faced with difficulties, consider, "What can I learn from this?" This shift in perspective can transform obstacles into opportunities for personal growth and development.

- **Speak Kindly to Yourself:** The internal dialogue you have with yourself is powerful. Replace negative self-talk like "I can't do this" with affirmations such as "I'm learning and improving every day." Your words shape your reality, so choose them wisely.

- **Spread Kindness:** Engaging in acts of kindness not only positively affects others, but also enhances your own emotional state. Simple gestures, like holding the door for someone or sending a compliment, create ripples of positivity.

- **Start Your Day with a Smile:** When you wake up, take a moment to think of something good. It could be the warmth of the sun, the smell of fresh coffee, or the love of your family. This simple act sets a positive tone for your whole day, shaping your outlook and interactions.

- **Start a Positivity Jar:** Write down positive events and experiences on slips of paper and place them in a jar. When you're feeling down, read through them to remind yourself of the good things in life.

- **Smile More:** Even if it feels forced at first, smiling can actually make you feel happier. It's a simple way to improve your mood and outlook.

- **Surround Yourself with Positive Reminders:** Use inspiring quotes, images, or objects to keep your mindset positive throughout the day. Visual cues can reinforce your commitment to a positive attitude.

- **Surround Yourself with Positive People:** Notice how a friend's mood can influence your own. Surround yourself with people who inspire and motivate you. Their optimism can fuel your own positive outlook.

- **Stay Curious:** Maintain a sense of wonder about the world. Curiosity keeps you engaged and excited about learning and discovering new things.

- **Take Breaks from Negative News:** While staying informed is important, constant exposure to negative news can affect your mood. Balance it with uplifting content to maintain a positive outlook.

- **Take Care of a Plant or Pet:** Nurturing a living thing can provide a sense of responsibility and joy. Plants and pets offer unconditional love and companionship.

- **Use Positive Affirmations:** Start each day with affirmations that reinforce your self-worth and capability. Phrases like "I am capable" or "I can handle whatever comes my way" or "I am taking positive steps to improve daily" set a positive tone for your day.

- **Visualize Success:** Use mental imagery to envision yourself overcoming challenges. Imagine the process and the feelings of achievement. Visualization can enhance your confidence and motivation.

- **Volunteer or Help Others:** When you help others, you experience a deep sense of purpose and contentment. Volunteering not only benefits those you help but also enhances your own well-being.

Embracing Positivity

Positivity is not just an attitude—it's a way of life that empowers you to navigate challenges with resilience, gratitude, and hope. By cultivating a positive mindset, you equip yourself with the tools to face life's ups and downs with grace and strength. Each positive thought is a seed growing into a reality shaped by optimism, joy, and fulfillment. From embracing setbacks as opportunities for growth to surrounding yourself with positive influences, every small step helps create a life rooted in well-being and success.

As you move forward, remember that positivity is a choice—a habit you can nurture daily. Whether it's practicing gratitude, use positive affirmations or adopting change with openness, your approach shapes not just your experience but also the lives of those around you. In the end, the strength of your positivity will determine the depth of your resilience, the joy in your heart, and the impact you leave behind.

Meaningful Insights:

- **Positivity is a Powerful Tool:** Your attitude shapes how you experience challenges, turning obstacles into opportunities for growth.
- **Mindset Shapes Reality**: Your thoughts influence your reality. A positive mindset can help transform your circumstances.
- **Practical Strategies for Positivity:** Simple practices such as starting your day with a smile, keeping a gratitude journal, and practicing positive self-talk can significantly improve your outlook and mental well-being.

9

Your Blueprint for Success

"The future belongs to those who believe in the beauty of their dreams."

—Eleanor Roosevelt

Setting goals is your roadmap to success. Ever feel like you're just drifting through life, unsure where you're headed? Maybe you have big dreams, but they seem so far away you don't know where to start. That's where setting goals and priorities comes in.

Think of goals as your life's GPS. Without them, you might wander around, see some cool stuff, but never really get to where you want to be. With clear goals, though, you've got direction. You know where you're going, and that's pretty exciting!

Begin with Your "Why"

Before you dive into setting goals, there's a crucial question you need to answer: Why are you pursuing these goals? Simon Sinek, in his book *Start with Why*[36], highlights the importance of knowing your purpose before anything else. When you understand your "why," everything you do has meaning. You're not just chasing success—you're pursuing something that speaks to your core values, something that matters deeply to you.

But this isn't a modern idea. Long before Sinek, philosopher Friedrich Nietzsche captured this sentiment perfectly when he said, *"If you have your why for life, you can get by with almost any how*[37]*."* Nietzsche's words remind us that having a strong reason behind our actions enables us to endure challenges. Your "why" becomes the fuel that keeps you moving forward when things get tough.

So, as you set your goals, start by reflecting on your deeper reasons. When you're clear on your "why", everything else falls into place.

The Art of Prioritizing

Once you've defined your "why," it's essential to prioritize. We all have lots of things we want to do, achieve, and experience. But let's face it—we can't do everything at once. That's where you need to figure out what really matters to you.

Prioritizing is like being the director of your own life movie. You get to decide which scenes are the most important, which ones can wait, and which ones can be cut altogether. It's about making choices that align with your values and long-term goals.

Practical Steps to Prioritize

Identify Your Core Values: Start by asking yourself some questions:

- What's most important to me in life? (Family, career, health, personal growth, etc.)
- What are my long-term goals?
- What actions will have the biggest positive impact on my goal?
- What am I passionate about?

Reflect and Align: Your answers to these questions can help guide your priorities. Maybe you realize that while you've been working long hours to get ahead in your career, what you really value most is spending time with your family. This realization might lead you to prioritize finding a better work-life balance. Remember, prioritizing doesn't mean you have to give up on certain goals. It just means you're choosing what to focus on right now. Other goals can wait their turn—they're not gone, just on the back burner for a while.

Set Clear and Achievable Goal

Not all goals are created equal. You want to set goals that are clear and achievable. Imagine telling yourself, "I want to be rich." That sounds nice, but what does it really mean? How will you know when you've achieved it? Instead, try something like, "I want to save $5,000 by the end of the year." See the difference? The second goal is clear—you know exactly what you're aiming for. And it's achievable—it might be a stretch, but it's not impossible.

When you set clear, achievable goals, you set yourself up for success. Each time you reach a goal, no matter how small, you get a boost of confidence. It's like your brain saying, "Hey, look at you go! You can do this!" And that feeling? It's pretty awesome. It makes you want to set and achieve more goals.

Breaking Down Big Dreams

Big dreams are great! Want to start your own business? Awesome! Want to travel the world? Go for it! But sometimes those big dreams can feel overwhelming. That's where breaking them down comes in handy. Let's say your big dream is to run a marathon. If you've never run before, the idea of running 26.2 miles might seem impossible. But what if you break it down? Maybe your first goal is to run a mile without stopping. Then aim for a 5K race. Then a 10K, a half marathon, and finally, the full marathon. Suddenly, that big dream doesn't seem so scary, right?

Breaking down your goals into smaller, manageable steps does two things. First, it makes the big goal feel more achievable. Second, it gives you a clear path to follow. You're not just saying, "I want to run a marathon someday." You're saying, "This month, I'm going to run my first 5K." It's specific, doable, and a step towards your bigger dream.

The Power of Saying No

Saying yes to one thing means saying no to something else. There are only so many hours in a day, right? So, when you say yes to staying late at work, you might be saying no to gym time or family dinner. When you say yes to binge-watching that new show, you might be saying no to working on your side hustle.

Learning to say no is a superpower. It's not about being negative—it's about being selective. It's about protecting your time and energy for the things that really matter to you. So, next time someone asks you to do something, pause for a moment.

Ask yourself: "Does this align with my priorities? Is this moving me closer to my goals?" If the answer is no, it's okay to politely decline.

The Magic of Vision Boards

Let's talk about something fun—vision boards! A vision board is like a collage of your dreams and goals. You gather images, words, and quotes that represent what you want to achieve and create a visual representation of your goals.

Why do this? Well, our brains love images. When you can see your goals, they feel more real and achievable. Plus, it's a great reminder of what you're working towards. You can create a physical vision board with magazines and a corkboard, or make a digital one using an app or website. Put your vision board somewhere you'll see it every day. Maybe it's by your desk, or maybe it's the background on your phone. The point is to keep your goals front and center in your mind.

Writing Down Your Goals

There's something magical about putting pen to paper. When you write down your goals, a few things happen:

- **They Become Real:** It's no longer just a thought in your head—it's out there in the world.
- **You're More Likely to Remember Them:** The act of writing helps cement the goals in your memory.
- **You Can Track Your Progress:** When you look back at what you've written, you can see how far you've come.

So, grab a journal, a notebook, or even just a piece of paper. Write down your goals. Be specific. Include deadlines if that helps you. And don't just write them once—make it a regular practice to review and rewrite your goals. This keeps them fresh in your mind and allows you to adjust them as needed.

Celebrating Small Wins

Here's something important: don't wait until you've achieved your big, ultimate goal to celebrate. Celebrate the small wins along the way! Remember how we talked about breaking down big goals into smaller steps? Each of those steps is worth celebrating. Did you save your first $100 towards your savings goal? Celebrate! Did you run your first mile without stopping? Do a happy dance! These celebrations serve a few purposes:

- **They Keep You Motivated:** It feels good to acknowledge your progress.
- **They Reinforce Positive Habits:** They remind you that you're making progress, even when the big goal still seems far away.

Your celebration doesn't have to be big. Maybe it's treating yourself to your favorite coffee drink or taking an evening off to watch your favorite movie. The important thing is to acknowledge your progress and give yourself a pat on the back.

Embracing Change and Overcoming Obstacles

It's totally okay to change your goals. In fact, it's normal and often necessary. As you grow and change, your priorities might shift. What seemed super important a year ago might not matter as much now. And that's okay! Regularly review your goals and priorities. Are they still in line with what you want in life? If not, don't be afraid to adjust them.

This isn't quitting—it's evolving. You're not giving up on your dreams; you're refining them based on what you've learned about yourself and the world. Maybe you set a goal to become a doctor, but along the way, you have discovered a passion for entrepreneurship. It's okay to shift gears and set new goals that align with this discovery. The important thing is to keep moving forward, keep growing, and keep working towards a life that fulfills you.

Working towards your goals isn't always smooth sailing. There will be obstacles. There will be days when you feel like giving up. That's normal, and it happens to everyone.

The key is to expect these tough times and have a plan for dealing with them. Here are a few strategies:

- **Remember Your "Why":** When things get tough, remind yourself why you set this goal in the first place.
- **Visualize Success:** Close your eyes and imagine how you'll feel when you achieve your goal. Let that good feeling motivate you.

- **Break It Down Even Further:** If a step towards your goal seems too hard, break it down into even smaller steps.
- **Seek Support:** Share your goals with friends or family who can cheer you on and hold you accountable.
- **Take a Break If Needed:** Sometimes stepping away for a bit can help you come back refreshed and re-motivated.

Remember, obstacles don't mean you're failing. They're just part of the process. Every time you overcome an obstacle, you're getting stronger and more resilient.

The Ripple Effect of Goals

When you set goals and work towards them, it doesn't just impact that one area of your life. It has a ripple effect that can positively influence other areas, too. Let's say you set a goal to exercise regularly. As you work towards this goal, you might notice that you have more energy at work. You might sleep better. Your mood might improve.

Suddenly, you're not just healthier—you're more productive, happier, and maybe even doing better in your relationships. Or maybe you set a goal to learn a new skill. As you work on this, you might discover hidden talents. You might meet new people who share your interests. Your confidence might grow as you master something new. The point is, when you actively work on improving one area of your life, other areas often improve too. It's like you're leveling up in the game of life!

Building a Support System

While setting and achieving goals is a personal endeavor, that doesn't mean you have to do it all alone. Having a support system can make a huge difference. This could be friends or family who encourage you and cheer you on. It could be a mentor who's achieved similar goals and can offer advice. It could be a coach who helps keep you accountable. Or it could be a group of people working towards similar goals—like a running club if you're training for a marathon, or a start-up group if you're working towards starting a new business.

Don't be afraid to share your goals with others. Sometimes just knowing that someone else is rooting for you can be incredibly motivating.

The Blueprint

Setting goals and priorities is like crafting the blueprint for the life you want to live. It's about taking control and making deliberate choices that align with your values and dreams. It's about being proactive rather than reactive. Life will always have its uncertainties and surprises, but with clear goals and priorities, you're better equipped to navigate them. You're not just drifting—you're steering the ship.

So, take a moment right now to think about your goals. Write them down. Break them into smaller steps. Prioritize what matters most. And don't forget to celebrate your progress along the way. You have the power to create a life that excites and fulfills you. It all starts with setting your sights on what you truly want and taking that first step towards it. Keep moving forward and stay focused.

Meaningful Insights:

- **Start with Your "Why":** Understanding your deeper purpose behind a goal is essential. This "why" serves as motivation during challenges and keeps you aligned with your values.
- **Prioritize What Matters**: Focus on what truly aligns with your core values and long-term vision. You can't achieve everything at once, so prioritize goals that have the biggest impact on your life.
- **Set Clear, Achievable Goals:** Vague goals won't lead to success. Instead, set specific, realistic goals with clear steps to help you stay focused and measure progress.

10

Navigating Life's Transition

Transitioning into Adulthood

Transitioning into adulthood is a significant milestone, marked by a blend of excitement and challenges. It signifies the beginning of a journey toward independence, where you navigate life on your own terms.

Financial Literacy

This transition involves mastering crucial skills, such as financial literacy, which is essential for achieving your dreams and ensuring long-term stability. Financial literacy is not merely about managing expenses, but about empowering yourself to make informed decisions that pave the way for both security and freedom. Envision the confidence that comes with being prepared for unexpected expenses or being able to save effectively for future goals.

Decision Making

However, financial independence is only one component of the broader transition. Decision-making plays a pivotal role in shaping your path. Cultivating critical thinking skills enables you to evaluate situations thoroughly and make choices that resonate with your values. Your values and ethics will act as your guiding compass, steering you through challenging choices and helping you remain steadfast in your beliefs. Recognizing the consequences of your actions is equally important.

Every decision you make creates a ripple effect, influencing not just your life but also those around you. For instance, missing a deadline can impact your team and erode their trust in you. Being aware of this interconnectedness fosters a sense of accountability that strengthens your character.

Personal Boundaries

As you mature, you'll encounter various challenges that test your ability to balance freedom with responsibility. Establishing personal boundaries is crucial; it defines what is acceptable in your life and what is not.

Time Management

Effective time management is another invaluable skill. Life often feels like a whirlwind of tasks, responsibilities, and opportunities. Learning to prioritize what truly matters will help you manage this chaos. Techniques such as making lists or using organizational apps can aid in staying focused and organized. Remember, effective time management isn't just about completing tasks; it's about creating space for what is most important, such as spending quality time with loved ones, pursuing hobbies that ignite your passion or dedicating time to personal growth and self-improvement.

Mentorship

Mentorship can significantly ease your transition into adulthood. Identifying and seeking out potential mentors can open doors to opportunities you might not have previously considered. Reflect on those you admire—individuals whose wisdom and experience inspire you. Learning from their experiences can offer invaluable insights and guidance. Seeking advice is not merely about gaining knowledge; it's about building connections that can last a lifetime. Everyone has a unique story, and these stories might impart lessons that textbooks alone cannot provide.

Entering the Workforce

The shift from student life to the workforce introduces new challenges and heightened stakes. The professional world can initially seem intimidating, but adopting a value-driven mindset will set you apart. By focusing on the positive impact you can bring to your organization, you not only enhance your contributions but also foster personal growth. This approach transforms work from a mere obligation into a meaningful pursuit. When you believe in your role and its significance, work becomes more than just a job—it becomes a purpose.

Research is a critical component of this transition. Before embarking on any job, immerse yourself in understanding the company's mission, vision, and goals. This knowledge will help you align your skills and prepare you for making meaningful contributions. By recognizing the company's challenges, you can position yourself as a problem-solver. Aligning your strengths with the company's needs establishes a powerful connection that can lead to success.

Setting clear, measurable goals is another essential step. Establish objectives that resonate with both your aspirations and the company's aims. Regularly tracking your progress keeps you accountable and motivated. It's akin to having a personal roadmap guiding you to your destination. Aim to surpass expectations; don't just fulfill the basic requirements. Seek opportunities to take initiative and demonstrate your commitment. Every time you exceed expectations, you build a reputation that others will notice and value.

Continuous improvement is a mindset that ensures you remain ahead in your career. Regularly seek feedback from managers or supervisors to identify areas for growth. Embrace constructive criticism as an opportunity to refine your skills. The goal is to evolve continually. Invest in your learning through professional development opportunities—whether it's attending workshops, obtaining certifications, or staying updated with industry trends. Networking with industry leaders can open doors and create opportunities you might not have previously considered.

Job Search

In your job search, identifying value-driven companies becomes crucial. Look for organizations that prioritize values, such as environmental stewardship, social responsibility, and strong governance (ESG criteria). Working for a company that genuinely cares about its employees' well-being will enhance your first job experience.

Crafting your Resume

Crafting an effective resume and cover letter is your chance to highlight your unique story. Tailor your resume to showcase relevant skills and experiences, distinguishing yourself from other candidates. Write a compelling cover letter that reflects your enthusiasm for the role and how your values align with the company's. This personal touch can make a significant difference, demonstrating your genuine interest in the opportunity.

Preparing for a Job Interview

Preparing for job interviews can be daunting, but practice can alleviate anxiety. Familiarize yourself with common interview questions and develop thoughtful responses. Thorough research on the company will enable you to ask questions that show your interest and alignment with their values. Dress appropriately and maintain a professional demeanor; first impressions are crucial.

Networking

Networking is an invaluable aspect of the job search. Utilize platforms like LinkedIn to connect with professionals in your desired field. Attend industry events, webinars, and career fairs to broaden your network and uncover potential opportunities. Seek out informational interviews to gain insights into potential employers and industry trends. Each connection you make can unlock new possibilities.

Adjusting to a New Work Environment

Stepping into your first job presents a learning curve that can be overwhelming. Navigating this transition requires patience and adaptability. Take the time to understand the company culture and workplace dynamics. Familiarize yourself with office protocols and the tools necessary for success. Building relationships with colleagues is crucial—introducing yourself and learning about their roles fosters a supportive network. Additionally, identifying key stakeholders in your projects can help streamline your work.

Setting realistic expectations is essential. Clarify your job responsibilities and performance goals with your manager. Don't hesitate to ask questions; this demonstrates your eagerness to align with the team's objectives. Set achievable short-term and long-term goals that inspire you to move forward while avoiding burnout.

Developing a strong work ethic is vital for long-term success. Show reliability by being punctual and meeting deadlines, which build trust. Take ownership of your work and strive for high quality in everything you do. Maintaining professionalism is equally important; dress appropriately and conduct yourself with integrity. Staying focused during work hours and minimizing distractions can significantly enhance your productivity.

Observing and listening are key skills in the workplace. Understand the stakeholders involved in your work, including colleagues, supervisors, and clients. Pay attention to their communication styles and priorities. Deep listening is valuable; listen more than you speak, especially when you're new. Asking questions not only improves your understanding but also demonstrates your interest and willingness to learn.

Learning from colleagues can accelerate your growth. Observe how experienced team members handle tasks and challenges. Use their approaches as opportunities to enhance your skills. Whether you learn from their successes or mistakes, each experience contributes to your development.

As you contemplate your career development, setting long-term goals will guide your path. Identify your strengths and interests to create a roadmap toward fulfillment.

Overcome Challenges at Workplace

Every workplace has its challenges, including dealing with toxic colleagues or incompetent bosses. Identifying toxic behavior is the first step in protecting your peace. Recognize signs of negativity, such as persistent criticism or undermining conduct. Distinguish between stress-related reactions and consistent toxicity. Maintain professionalism when dealing with toxic colleagues; avoid gossip, set boundaries, and communicate assertively if necessary. If their behavior impacts your work, seek support from HR or a trusted mentor.

Handling incompetent bosses can be challenging, but focusing on your performance and maintaining a positive attitude can help. Document important communications and decisions to protect yourself. Look for alternative mentors within the organization who can offer guidance. If the situation becomes intolerable, consider discussing your concerns with HR or exploring other opportunities within the company.

Understanding workplace dynamics is crucial. Recognize and adapt to different corporate cultures to thrive. Professional etiquette and effective communication with colleagues and superiors foster a positive work environment. Building strong professional relationships is key; teamwork and collaboration often lead to greater success.

Managing Work Relates Stress

Managing work-related stress is essential for your well-being. Identifying stressors and developing coping mechanisms will help you navigate challenges. Seeking support when needed demonstrates strength and resilience.

Creating Side Hustle

Developing a side hustle alongside your job is more than just a practical move; it's a powerful investment in your future. As it matures, this endeavor becomes a gateway to freedom, allowing you to step back or make bold life changes with confidence. Think of it as your personal sandbox—a space where you can test ideas, build resilience, and hone essential skills that keep you sharp and adaptable in today's fast-changing world. By cultivating a project outside the bounds of your day-to-day work, you're carving a path aligned with your values and aspirations, setting the stage for a professional path that's not only rewarding but also deeply fulfilling.

Climbing the Corporate Ladder in a Modern Business World: A Non-Linear Journey

The traditional concept of climbing the corporate ladder—a straightforward, linear ascent from entry-level positions to executive roles—has evolved dramatically in recent years. Today, the corporate landscape is characterized by complexity, influenced by rapid technological advancements, including artificial intelligence (AI), globalization, changing organizational structures, evolving workforce expectations, increasing geopolitical tensions, and the ongoing energy transition.

Innovation and Technological Advancement

In today's fast-paced world, technology isn't just advancing; it's revolutionizing. The companies that thrive aren't merely keeping up—they're disrupting, redefining, and transforming

Apple and BlackBerry provide a classic study in contrast: Apple built its empire by boldly creating new categories, blending sleek design with seamless, user-friendly experiences. The iPhone wasn't just a phone; it was the beginning of a connected ecosystem—the App Store, iCloud, and beyond—that locked in customer loyalty and set a high bar for competitors[38].

In contrast, BlackBerry, though a giant in its early days with its secure email and iconic keyboard, couldn't break away from its comfort zone. Its incremental improvements became obsolete in the face of Apple's sweeping vision. BlackBerry's downfall serves as a powerful reminder: even the strongest can falter without adaptability[39].

Fast forward to today, and artificial intelligence (AI) has taken the spotlight. Companies like Google, Microsoft, and OpenAI are redefining what's possible, pushing AI to automate, predict, and perform in ways once limited to human imagination. Industries from healthcare to finance are being reimagined as AI takes on roles from analyzing data to enhancing customer interactions[40] [41] [42] [43]. Those who recognize AI's potential and integrate it into their operations are emerging as leaders, while others risk being left behind.

This isn't just about technology; it's about embracing change itself. Whether it's Tesla shaking up the auto industry, Netflix reinventing entertainment, or Amazon reshaping the way we shop, the message is clear: innovation isn't a choice; it's a necessity. To stay relevant, adapt, disrupt, and be ready to reinvent yourself. Only then can you secure your place in a landscape that never stops moving.

Globalisation

Globalization has reshaped the business landscape, unleashing a wave of intense competition alongside unprecedented opportunities. A key driver of this transformation is the establishment of Free Trade Areas (FTAs). Examples include the European Union (EU) Single Market[44], ASEAN Free Trade Area (AFTA)[45], Comprehensive and Progressive Agreement for Trans-Pacific Partnership (CPTPP)[46], and ASEAN-China Free Trade Area (ACFTA)[47]. These agreements remove barriers like tariffs and import quotas, paving the way for smoother, faster trade across borders. The result? An economic environment that encourages collaboration, integration, and growth among member countries.

For businesses, FTAs open new doors to international markets, dramatically reducing operational costs and eliminating restrictions that once held companies back. With broader access to global customer bases and diverse, cost-effective supply chains, companies can scale operations internationally with an agility that previous generations could only imagine. This reach allows them to meet worldwide demand with heightened efficiency, elevating both their capacity and competitive advantage.

But these open doors come with higher stakes. International players pour into local markets, raising the bar for all, pushing businesses to innovate, refine operations, and set new quality standards. The pressure to compete globally sharpens a company's edge, turning challenges into catalysts for growth in today's fast-paced, interconnected economy.

Recent developments in globalization underscore the complexity of this interconnectedness. New agreements increasingly address digital trade, environmental sustainability, and labor standards, recognizing that the modern economy goes beyond physical goods. For instance, the CPTPP[48] and recent updates to agreements within the EU[49] prioritize not only trade but also data privacy and environmental responsibility—fundamentals of a sustainable, future-oriented economy. Additionally, the landmark global accords like the Paris Agreement[50] reflect a collective initiative towards reducing environmental impact, highlighting that trade agreements now intersect with global climate goals, marking an urgency towards responsible globalization.

Understanding globalization and its latest trends is crucial to navigating a landscape that's both competitive and collaborative. In a world where borders are less visible than ever, positioning yourself as a globally savvy player ensures that you're ready to seize new career opportunities, engage with cross-border partnerships, and stay resilient in the dynamic, interconnected world we inhabit.

Geopolitical Tensions

Geopolitical tensions have added layers of uncertainty, requiring companies to be more agile and innovative, and making it essential for professionals to differentiate themselves and add unique value. For example, the recent ongoing geopolitical tensions between Hamas and Israel have had significant impacted global shipping routes, particularly through the Red Sea, a critical maritime passage.

Increased security risks and disruptions have led to changes in shipping routes, as the Red Sea has become less accessible. This shift has caused delays and increased costs for global trade, affecting businesses that rely on this vital route for transporting goods[51] [52]. The combined effects of these geopolitical and logistical challenges underscore the far-reaching impact of regional conflicts on global commerce.

By understanding the broader impact of geopolitical events, you equip yourself to make informed decisions and position yourself as a proactive, strategic professional in an unpredictable world.

Agility and Adaptability in Career Success

The path to career success now requires adaptability, continuous learning, and strategic decision-making. Besides professional development, awareness of both macro and micro environmental factors—such as global economic trends, technological advancements, and industry-specific shifts is crucial. By adopting a non-linear career path, you can seize opportunities that align with your strengths and aspirations, ultimately leading to a more fulfilling and successful career. The modern corporate ladder may be unpredictable, but with the right mindset and strategies, you can chart a path to the top.

Consider the following strategies:

- **Lateral Moves for Skill Development:** Lateral moves involve transitioning to a different role at the same level. These moves allow you to diversify your skill set, gain new experiences, and build a more robust professional portfolio. For example, moving from a marketing role to a business development position can broaden your understanding of how different departments contribute to the organization's success.

- **Continuous Learning and Adaptability:** Staying relevant in your field means regularly updating your skills, embracing new technologies, and being open to change. Whether through formal or informal education or on-the-job training, continuous learning ensures that you remain competitive and adaptable in a rapidly evolving environment.

- **Networking Across Boundaries:** Building relationships across different industries, regions, and cultures can open doors to new opportunities and provide valuable insights. Networking by connecting with professionals worldwide through social media, industry events, and virtual conferences can expand your horizons and introduce you to new perspectives.

- **Enhance Your Understanding of Micro and Macro Environmental Factor:** Developing awareness of both macro and micro environmental factors is essential for strategic decision-making. Macro factors include broad influences, such as economic conditions, political and legal environments, technological advancements, sociocultural trends, and environmental issues. Micro factors involve more immediate aspects, like industry competitors, customer needs, supplier relationships, market intermediaries, and internal company dynamics. Understanding these factors helps in anticipating changes, adapting strategies, and making informed decisions.

- **Taking Calculated Risks:** This might include switching industries, joining a startup, or pursuing a new specialization. While these decisions can be daunting, they can also lead to significant career growth and personal fulfillment. The key is to assess the risks carefully, consider the potential benefits, and make informed choices that align with your long-term goals.

The Entrepreneurial Path

Entrepreneurship is a path you might consider at some point in your life. It's more than just starting a business; it's about building something meaningful, creating value, and making a positive impact on society. This endeavor requires vision, courage, and an unwavering commitment to overcoming obstacles.

However, entrepreneurship also comes with its share of risks. Financial uncertainty, market volatility, and the possibility of failure are all part of the entrepreneurial landscape. Yet, for those who embrace these challenges, the rewards can be substantial—not only in terms of financial success but also in the deep satisfaction of turning dreams into reality and leaving a lasting legacy. Balancing risk with innovation and resilience is key to navigating this complex yet rewarding journey.

The Entrepreneurial Life Cycle

According to the Global Entrepreneur Institute[53], the entrepreneurial life cycle is divided into seven stages, each requiring distinct approaches and strategies:

1. **Opportunity Recognition:** This initial stage involves identifying and assessing potential business ideas. Entrepreneurs must evaluate market needs and feasibility to ensure their ideas have a solid foundation.

2. **Opportunity Focusing:** In this stage, the concept is refined and validated. Entrepreneurs develop a clear business model, conduct market research, and create prototypes or proof-of-concept to test the viability of their ideas.

3. **Commitment of Resources:** This stage involves creating a comprehensive business plan and allocating the necessary resources. Entrepreneurs commit

financial capital, whether from personal savings or external funding sources, along with time and effort to bring their business idea to life.

4. **Market Entry:** At this point, the business starts making sales and generating revenue. The focus is on gaining traction, establishing a customer base, and achieving initial success.

5. **Full Launch and Growth:** This stage marks a decision point where the entrepreneur decides whether to scale the business. It involves expanding operations, increasing market reach, and optimizing business processes.

6. **Maturity and Expansion:** In this stage, the business has become a market leader and focuses on sustained growth and professional management. Strategic planning and continuous improvement are essential to maintain competitive advantage.

7. **Liquidity Event:** The final stage involves exiting the business, typically through an Initial Public Offering (IPO), Private Equity Investment, or Trade Sale. This stage requires careful planning to maximize returns and ensure a successful transition.

Each stage of the entrepreneurial life cycle demands a specific mindset, skill set, and execution capabilities. Entrepreneurs must adapt to changing conditions, manage resources effectively, and lead their teams through various challenges. Success requires a balance of visionary thinking and practical execution, along with a deep understanding of the market and the ability to inspire and guide others.

From Concept to Expansion: Navigating the Entrepreneurial Terrain with the "Nail It, Scale It, Sail It" Strategic Framework

Lorendana Padurean's analogy of "Nail It, Scale It, Sail It[54]" offers a nature-inspired perspective on the entrepreneurial path:

- **Nail It Stage**: A Journey of Speed and Frugality: This phase emphasizes rapid validation and refinement of the business idea, much like navigating through a dense jungle. Entrepreneurs focus on testing the market, solving problems quickly, and establishing their brand. The team is small, agile, and driven by a "Yes, we can" attitude. Efficiency and adaptability are crucial as they work to establish a solid foundation for the business.

- **Scale It Stage**: A Journey of Growth and Agility: As the business moves beyond the initial phase, much like ascending a steep mountain after surviving the jungle, the focus shifts to growth and optimization, Entrepreneurs map out new opportunities, refine processes, and scale operations. Strategic micro-pivots and targeted market segmentation become essential.

Building a strong brand and maintaining a culture of collective responsibility are key components of this stage.

- **Sail It Stage:** A Journey of Endurance and Sustainability: In this final phase, the focus is on sustaining long-term success. Entrepreneurs navigate complex and unpredictable conditions, ensuring resilience and adaptability. The team's role becomes more structured, with an emphasis on maintaining stability and continuous improvement. Endurance and strategic thinking are essential as the business strives for sustainable growth.

Case Study - gojek: Evolving Leadership Through the Stages of "Nail It, Scale It, Sail It"

gojek is a pioneering force in the Southeast Asia tech industry, recognized as the first Indonesian unicorn company. Its impact extends beyond the business realm, as it became the only company in Southeast Asia to be included in Fortune's "50 Companies That Changed the World," ranking 17th in 2017 and 11th in 2019. By June 2020, gojek had amassed approximately 170 million users across Southeast Asia, underscoring its significant influence and widespread adoption[55].

In a CNBC interview[56], the founder of gojek, Nadiem Makarim, shared insights into his leadership journey, which perfectly illustrates the "Nail It, Scale It, Sail It" model in action.

Reflecting on the early days of gojek, Makarim explained, *"My leadership style at the beginning was a lot more assertive, a little of micromanagement and a lot more I want to control everything."* This approach at the "Nail It" phase, while demanding, was necessary to navigate the complexities of a startup environment, where rapid decision-making and close control can be critical to success.

As gojek grew, Makarim's leadership style evolved to meet the new challenges of the "Scale It" phase. He recognized the need to adapt, noting, *"As the company scaled, and we had more and more talent and we had more and more things to do, that feeling of having to control every single outcome began to frustrate me and it wore me out."* This realization led him to shift his mindset, recognizing that empowering teams closer to the ground allowed for better solutions and greater efficiency. This shift is a key element of scaling successfully—moving from hands-on management to empowering others to take ownership and lead within their areas of expertise.

Makarim emphasized the necessity of evolving leadership styles as the company matured to the "Sail It" phase: *"If you don't evolve your leadership style for where your company is at the moment, then you will render yourself useless very quickly."* His experience underscores the importance of adapting leadership approaches to match the changing needs of the company—a critical insight for entrepreneurs navigating the final stages of their journey.

Padurean's analogy emphasizes that each stage of entrepreneurship requires a different mindset and skill set, reflecting the complexities and evolving nature of the journey at different stages. Makarim's journey at gojek exemplifies this, as he adapted his mindset and leadership style through the "Nail It, Scale It, Sail It" phases, highlighting the need for continuous growth and evolution in leadership to ensure long-term success.

The Art of Leadership

Guiding Your Path in Corporate or Entrepreneurial Journeys

Whether you're climbing the corporate ladder or venturing into entrepreneurship, leadership is a crucial component of your journey. The responsibility of leadership goes beyond personal ambitions; it involves meeting the expectations and demands placed upon you.

As stated in Luke 12:48 *"From everyone who has been given much, much will be demanded; and from the one who has been entrusted with much, much more will be asked."* This highlights the expectation that those in positions of power or influence are held to higher standards and must deliver on the responsibilities entrusted to them.

Integrity, Resilience and Strategic Vision

Leadership involves not just directing and influencing others, but also embodying principles of integrity, resilience, and strategic vision. As Lord Acton famously said, *"Power corrupts and absolute power corrupts absolutely*[57]*."* This quote underscores the importance of ethical leadership and the need for self-awareness and accountability at all levels.

The lessons we have shared on self-reflection, deep listening, purposeful communication, moral compass, integrity, change, and resilience are all essential ingredients for effective leadership. These elements form the foundation of a leader's ability to inspire, guide, and make impactful decisions. Embracing these principles ensures that leadership is not just about achieving results, but also about fostering a positive and ethical environment that promotes growth and respect.

Effective Leadership

Effective leadership in both corporate and entrepreneurial contexts entails fostering innovation, managing change, and prioritizing emotional intelligence and diversity. Inspiring and guiding teams toward a shared vision while motivating individuals to achieve their potential and fostering collaboration and trust are key responsibilities. Leaders must excel in financial management, crisis response, and stakeholder relations, while also adeptly managing risks, focusing on customer needs, and allocating resources efficiently. Building networks, developing robust marketing strategies, and ensuring legal compliance are essential. Embracing sustainability and maintaining adaptability are crucial for long-term success and resilience in a dynamic business environment.

More importantly, effective leadership in modern organizations demands a mindset shift toward agility, inclusivity, and a holistic approach. According to a McKinsey article titled *New Leadership for a New Era of Thriving Organizations*[58], leaders should make five critical shifts to meet today's complex organizational demands:

- **From Directive to Empowering Leadership:** Transitioning from giving directives to empowering teams promotes autonomy and innovation.
- **From Controlling to Enabling Execution:** Shifting from strict process control to enable execution fosters agility and responsiveness.
- **From Managing to Coaching:** Moving from task management to coaching individuals supports personal and professional growth.
- **From Operating in Silos to Collaborating Across Boundaries**: Breaking down silos and encouraging cross-functional collaboration enhances organizational agility.
- **From Self-focused to Stakeholder-focused Leadership:** Expanding focus from self-interest in considering all stakeholders aligns with sustainable and inclusive growth.

Lastly, it's crucial to remember that not ensuring compliance can have severe repercussions for both the business and individuals in the long term. I often emphasize the principle of "*ignorantia juris non excusat*" (ignorance of the law is no excuse[59]), a legal maxim that holds a person accountable for violating a law, regardless of their awareness of its existence or content. Compliance is not just about following regulations; it is about safeguarding the integrity and sustainability of both personal and business endeavors.

Ethical Leadership

History is filled with examples where leaders' short-sighted decisions and unethical actions have led to significant downfalls. A notable case is Enron[60] [61], once a top energy company, which collapsed due to extensive accounting fraud and unethical business practices. The company's leadership, driven by a quest for profit and power, engaged in deceptive activities that ultimately resulted in its bankruptcy and a massive loss of investor confidence.

The repercussions of Enron's failure extended beyond the company, leading to the closure of its accounting firm, Arthur Andersen. Arthur Andersen was implicated in the scandal for its role in facilitating and covering up Enron's fraudulent actions, demonstrating the deep and widespread consequences of unethical conduct.

Similarly, the case of Lehman Brothers[62], the fourth-largest investment bank in the United States with 25,000 employees worldwide, illustrates how unethical risk-taking and inadequate oversight can precipitate a financial crisis. The bank's aggressive pursuit of high-risk investments, coupled with its lack of transparency in financial dealings, contributed to its dramatic failure. With $639 billion in assets, its collapse triggered the global financial crisis of 2008, demonstrating the far-reaching consequences of irresponsible leadership and decision-making in the financial sector.

Wirecard[63] [64], once hailed as a rising star and the pride of German FinTech, highlights the disastrous impact of unethical leadership. The company's leadership orchestrated an elaborate fraud that misled investors and regulators about its financial health. This scandal, involving fraudulent activities that spanned two decades, was marked by fabricated financial statements, a missing €1.9 billion, misleading audits, and deceptive business practices, particularly in its international expansion. It caused national embarrassment for Germany and led to Wirecard's insolvency on June 25, 2020. This case not only damaged investor confidence, but also exposed significant regulatory failures and governance issues within the financial industry.

The collapses of Enron, Lehman Brothers, and Wirecard reveal the catastrophic fallout of unethical leadership. These high-profile downfalls underscore the vital importance of ethical decision-making and the dangers inherent in greed and corruption. They serve as powerful reminders that integrity and transparency aren't just ideals—they are essential pillars for sustainable leadership and lasting success.

Building Your Team

A successful team is built on shared values and commitment to integrity. As Michael Jordan said, *"Talent wins games, but teamwork and intelligence win championships[65]."* This highlights the importance of teamwork and the need for individuals who share your ethical standards and values.

Another famous quote that exemplifies true leadership is from Nelson Mandela, who once said, *"What counts in life is not the mere fact that we have lived. It is what difference we have made to the lives of others that will determine the significance of the life we lead[66]."* This quote underscores the importance of building a team that is not just skilled, but also committed to making a positive impact.

Leadership is about more than just guiding others; it's about fostering an environment where every team member is motivated by a shared purpose to make a meaningful difference. By focusing on these principles, you can cultivate a team that embodies integrity and works together to achieve long-term success.

Echoing this sentiment, Queen Elizabeth II observed, *"I know of no single formula for success. But over the years, I have observed that some attributes of leadership are universal and are often about finding ways of encouraging people to combine their efforts, their talents, their insights, their enthusiasm, and their inspiration to work together[67]."* This statement highlights the universal nature of leadership qualities and the importance of collaboration in achieving collective success.

By encouraging your team to combine their strengths and work together harmoniously, you can build a cohesive and dynamic unit that is capable of achieving great things.

Applying Tuckman's Stages of Group Development to Team Formation

One of the most popular models for understanding team formation is Tuckman's stages of group development[68], first introduced by Bruce Tuckman in 1965. This model has been widely discussed in academic and management journals for its applicability in various organizational settings. Tuckman's model shares similarities with M. Scott Peck's community building model, though they are applied in different contexts. Both frameworks aim to guide groups through a series of stages to achieve a cohesive, effective, and well-functioning team or community.

Here's how these stages can apply to effective team formation:

Stage 1: Forming Stage

This initial stage is characterized by orientation and acquaintance. Team members learn about the project and their responsibilities, and interactions are typically polite and exploratory. The focus is on understanding the tasks and how the team will work together. This stage is crucial for setting the tone of teamwork and establishing clear goals and expectations.

Application: Leaders should focus on facilitating introductions, clearly defining roles and objectives, and creating a supportive environment that encourages open communication. This helps in building a foundation for trust and collaborative work.

Stage 2: Storming Stage

During this stage, the team encounters conflict and confrontation as members express their individual perspectives and challenge each other's ideas. This is a critical phase where team dynamics are tested and issues of hierarchy and power are addressed.

Application: Effective management of this stage involves mediating conflicts, ensuring respectful communication, and guiding the team towards a constructive resolution of disagreements. Leadership is crucial here to help the team transition to more stable dynamics by encouraging openness and reinforcing the team's shared goals.

Stage 3: Norming Stage

After navigating through conflicts, the team starts to consolidate around agreed norms and values. Cooperation emerges as team members adjust their behaviors and work processes to support collective performance.

Application: To foster this stage, leaders should emphasize team norms and values, recognize and reward collaborative behavior, and encourage team members to share responsibility for the team's success. This promotes a sense of unity and shared purpose.

Stage 4: Performing Stage

Performing Stage: Teams reach this stage when they have established stable relationships and can execute tasks efficiently and effectively without inappropriate conflict. The focus is on collective performance and achieving the team's goals.

Application: In this high-functioning phase, leaders can delegate substantial responsibility to the team, relying on its members to take initiative and lead in various aspects. It's also important to sustain team health through ongoing development and challenges.

Fostering Team Growth and Sustaining Excellence

Each stage of team development serves a specific function in the maturation of a team and has applications that can help facilitate the transition to the next level of performance. Recognizing and effectively managing each stage is essential for leaders to maximize team productivity and cohesion.

Allowing your team to progress through these stages is crucial. Once you reach the performing stage, it's important to focus on retaining your team to sustain high performance and success.

Understanding the strengths and weaknesses of each team member is essential. Take time to know them as individuals beyond their technical skills and contributions—understand what motivates them, what is important to them, their dreams, and their background. Focusing on bringing out the best in your team and helping them improve their areas of weakness fosters a supportive and effective work environment.

As President Theodore Roosevelt famously said, *"No one cares how much you know until they know how much you care*[69]*."* This quote underscores the importance of empathy and genuine concern in leadership.

Steering Through Difficult Decisions

In your journey as a leader, you will often face difficult decisions that can significantly impact the future of your organization. These decisions may involve financial constraints, ethical dilemmas, or strategic shifts. Sometimes, all the options available may seem bad, making this the most painful and lonely part of leadership. As a leader, you will often face solitude because you bear the ultimate responsibility for decisions and outcomes, and this burden can be heavy.

As Sir Ernest Shackleton succinctly quoted, *"Loneliness is the penalty of leadership, but the man who has to make the decisions is assisted greatly if he feels that there is no uncertainty in the minds of those who follow him, and that his orders will be carried out confidently and in expectation of success[70]."*

Effective leadership, team-building, and decision-making are deeply interconnected. It is not just about making tough choices; it is about guiding your team through with clarity and confidence. By adhering to ethical principles, fostering strong team dynamics, and making informed, principled choices, leaders and entrepreneurs can navigate complex challenges and guide their ventures toward success. As Shackleton's insight acknowledges, although leadership can be isolating, its true strength lies in the ability to inspire certainty and confidence among those you lead, even in the face of difficult decisions.

To navigate these challenges effectively, consider the following guiding principles:

- **Clarity of Purpose:** Keep the organization's broader mission and vision in mind. Ensure that each decision aligns with long-term goals and core values.

- **Data-Driven Analysis:** Make decisions based on thorough analysis and relevant data. Carefully weigh potential risks and benefits to make well-informed choices.

- **Ethical Considerations**: Assess the ethical implications of each decision. Prioritize transparency and integrity to build and maintain trust with stakeholders.

- **Stakeholder Impact:** Evaluate how decisions will affect all stakeholders, including employees, customers, and investors. Aim for solutions that balance and respect the interests of diverse groups.

- **Resilience and Adaptability:** Be ready to adapt decisions as new information or circumstances arise. Flexibility is essential for navigating uncertainty and ensuring long-term success.

- **Appreciation of History:** Understand the historical context of your industry and organization. Learning from past successes and failures can provide valuable insights that inform current decision-making and help avoid repeating mistakes.

- **Mastery of Competing and Complex Issues:** Develop the ability to navigate and balance competing priorities and interests. A leader must skillfully manage diverse and often conflicting demands to achieve the best outcomes for the organization.

As you embark on your own journey as a leader, remember that the path will not always be easy, and the weight of your decisions may often feel heavy. But know this: true leadership is not about having all the answers, but about making choices that are guided by integrity, compassion, and wisdom. In those moments when the road seems lonely, let your values be your compass, and trust that by leading with courage and conviction, you will inspire others to follow with confidence. Always remember, you carry within you the strength and resilience to overcome any challenge.

Transition from Singlehood to Marriage

Marriage signifies a move from individualism to partnership. The commitment extends beyond personal well-being to include the happiness and welfare of your spouse. This partnership involves sharing both the burdens and joys of life, making collaborative decisions, and supporting each other's dreams and aspirations. Preparation for marriage involves open discussions about expectations, future goals, and addressing any pre-wedding anxieties. Transparency in sharing feelings helps strengthen the bond between partners.

Trust and honesty become foundational elements in strengthening your relationship. By employing the lessons from *Chapter 3, Growing Together: Navigating Relationships*, you can foster growth and ensure that your relationship remains resilient and supportive.

Starting a Family

Starting a family is one of the most consequential decisions in life, carrying profound emotional, financial, and physical implications. It is essential to evaluate your readiness in these areas before embarking on this significant step. Parenthood is a journey marked by immense joys and inevitable challenges, each stage offering new experiences and learning opportunities. Understanding your child's developmental stages—from infancy to adolescence—is crucial for fostering their growth and well-being.

As a parent, your responsibilities extend beyond yourself; you become a pivotal influence on another person's life. Children are keen observers, and much of their learning comes from observing the actions, behaviors, and attitudes of the adults around them. Every action you take, every word you speak, and your general demeanor significantly shape your child's experiences, values, and worldview. The foundation you lay during these formative years is critical for their emotional and psychological health, affecting their future relationships, self-esteem, and overall outlook on life.

Balancing work and family life is a delicate task that demands conscious effort, patience, and a clear sense of priorities. Setting realistic goals and establishing clear priorities can guide you in managing both your professional and personal demands effectively. In today's fast-paced world, flexibility and adaptability are indispensable tools for navigating this complex landscape. When conflicts arise—whether between work commitments and family obligations or within the family itself—addressing them constructively and seeking solutions that honor both your career and family life is essential for maintaining harmony and fulfillment in both areas.

Raising children can be overwhelming, and amidst these responsibilities, it's important not to lose sight of your relationship with your partner. Making time for each other is crucial in maintaining a strong, supportive partnership, which in turn creates a stable and nurturing environment for your children.

Self-care is not merely a luxury but a fundamental necessity for sustaining your well-being and effectiveness as a partner, parent and professional. Recognizing early signs of burnout, such as fatigue, irritability, and a sense of being overwhelmed, is crucial for maintaining your mental, emotional, and physical health. Incorporating self-care practices into your daily routine—whether through exercise, meditation, or quiet reflection—helps recharge your energy and spirit, enabling you to meet the demands of your roles with resilience.

Effective time management and setting boundaries are key strategies that allow you to prioritize your health and well-being without guilt. By taking care of yourself, you ensure that you are in the best position to care for your family and succeed in your career.

Midlife

A Time for Renewal and Reflection

Entering midlife offers a unique opportunity for reflection and renewal. Celebrating personal and professional milestones reminds you of your journey and achievements. Reassessing your goals and future aspirations provides clarity and direction for the years ahead. Change is an inevitable part of life, and managing career transitions and coping with empty nest syndrome requires resilience and adaptability. Embracing these changes can lead to new opportunities and personal growth.

Finding purpose during midlife can be incredibly fulfilling. Rediscovering passions and hobbies that bring you joy can rejuvenate your spirit. Exploring new interests keeps your mind engaged and adds excitement to your life. Considering alternative career paths or entrepreneurial ventures can spark creativity and passion. Continuous learning and growth are essential at any stage of life.

The Voyage of Life

Life unfolds in a series of chapters, each contributing to the person you become. As you move through these chapters, embrace the challenges, celebrate the victories, and cherish the connections you make. Your journey is uniquely yours, and with every step, you have the power to create a meaningful legacy that inspires others. So, move forward with courage, keep learning, and remember that every moment counts.

Meaningful Insights:

- **Navigating Adulthood Requires Independence and Accountability**: Transitioning into adulthood involves mastering financial literacy, decision-making, and time management, while taking responsibility for your actions and understanding the interconnectedness of decisions.

- **Career Transitions Demand Preparation and Continuous Growth**: Moving from education to the workforce, or between jobs, requires aligning personal values with organizational goals, continuous learning, and building strong networks to adapt to new challenges and environments.

- **Leadership and Entrepreneurship Evolve Through Stages:** Whether in corporate or entrepreneurial settings, leadership must adapt at different stages, from hands-on control to empowering others and managing long-term growth. Successful transitions in leadership involve ethical decision-making and team-building.

- **Marriage and Family Life Require Communication and Balance**: Transitioning from singlehood to marriage and starting a family requires clear communication, mutual support, and shared values. Balancing personal and professional responsibilities while maintaining self-care is essential for thriving in these new roles.

- **Midlife Offers a Chance for Renewal and Reflection:** As life progresses, midlife is an opportunity to reassess goals, rediscover passions, and embrace new directions. Continuous growth, adaptability, and accepting life's changes are key to thriving through midlife transitions.

11

The Power of Lifelong Learning

"Education is the most powerful weapon which you can use to change the world."

—Nelson Mandela

You already know how important learning is. From the time you're a child, you're told to pay attention in school, aim for good grades, and take your education seriously. But have you ever stopped to think about why education matters so much? And is school the only place where learning happens?

In this chapter, let's explore why education remains invaluable throughout your life. Schools are important, but learning can happen in many ways. Once you embrace education and lifelong learning, it will shape your life for the better, allowing you to grow continuously and open new doors.

A Path to Empowerment

Think about the last time you learned something new. Maybe it was a fascinating fact about the universe, a delicious recipe, or even a new dance step. How did it feel? The excitement of learning something fresh—that's the transformative power of education!

Education isn't just about memorizing facts or passing exams. It's about expanding your mind, unlocking new perspectives, and fostering personal growth. It allows us to see the world in ways we hadn't imagined before.

Consider your brain as a muscle—the more you challenge it, the stronger it gets. Each new piece of information exercises your brain, making you more creative, capable, and better at problem-solving.

The benefits of education extend far beyond individual growth. An educated community leads to better decision-making, tolerance for different viewpoints, and the ability to address complex challenges.

Nelson Mandela once said, *"Education is the most powerful weapon which you can use to change the world."* Mandela's story—captured in his memoir *Long Walk to Freedom*[71]—is a testament to how learning can uplift individuals and societies.

The Role of Formal Education

When most people think of education, they think of school—classrooms, teachers, textbooks. This is called formal education, and while it plays a crucial role, it is only one piece of the learning puzzle.

Formal education provides essential building blocks: reading, writing, arithmetic—skills necessary for lifelong learning. But beyond the basics, school teaches us how to think critically, how to analyze information, how to collaborate with others. These are the skills that will stay with you far beyond graduation, no matter your chosen career path.

In school, you also have the chance to explore a variety of subjects. You might discover a love for mathematics, develop a talent for music, or ignite a passion for literature. School is a place of discovery, where you can identify what excites and motivates you.

More than academic learning, schools foster social development. They bring people from different backgrounds together, teaching us how to work as part of a team, navigate social dynamics, and form meaningful relationships.

Perhaps the most pivotal element of formal education is the role teachers play. A great teacher doesn't simply impart knowledge; they inspire, challenge, and encourage you to believe in your potential. Most of us can recall a teacher who had a profound impact on our lives, helping to shape the person we've become.

However, formal education is not the only path to learning. While schools offer a structured environment for knowledge, the real journey of learning extends far beyond the classroom.

Lifelong Learning
Beyond the Classroom

Learning doesn't end with a degree. In fact, much of the most important learning occurs outside the school walls. This is where the concept of lifelong learning comes in—remaining curious and open to new ideas throughout your life.

Socrates, the ancient Greek philosopher, once said, *"I am wiser than this man; it is likely that neither of us knows anything worthwhile, but he thinks he knows something, when he does not, whereas when I do not know, neither do I think I know,"* recorded in *The Apology*[72] by Plato.

Socrates taught that recognizing one's ignorance is the first step toward wisdom—a reminder that even our own beliefs deserve regular reflection. Are there any assumptions you hold that could benefit from deeper examination?

True wisdom comes not from knowing everything, but from the recognition that there is always more to learn. Lifelong learning allows us to continue growing as individuals, long after our formal education ends.

Here are a few ways you can continue learning outside of school:

- **Read Books and Articles:** Books open worlds of knowledge. Whether it's fiction, non-fiction, or articles, reading is one of the most powerful ways to expand your understanding.

- **Watch Educational Videos**: Platforms like YouTube provide vast resources for learning. From complex theories to practical skills, there's something for everyone.

- **Take Online Courses:** Many websites offer accessible courses on a wide range of topics. Whether it's coding, art, or history, you can learn at your own pace.

- **Learn from Others**: People around us have so much to teach. Be open to listening and learning from their experiences.

- **Explore New Activities**: Stepping out of your comfort zone is one of the best ways to learn. Whether it's cooking, painting, or gardening, new experiences bring new lessons.

- **Travel**: Exploring new places broadens your perspective and exposes you to different cultures and ways of life.

- **Pursue Hobbies:** Engaging in activities that spark joy, such as playing an instrument or building a project, offers opportunities for learning in a fun, fulfilling way.

- **Work Experiences**: Every job, even a part-time one, teaches valuable skills, from teamwork to leadership.

Lifelong learning isn't just about accumulating knowledge—it's about continuous self-improvement. As you learn, you become more adaptable, open-minded, and better equipped to tackle the world's challenges.

Exploring New Ideas

One of the most exciting parts of lifelong learning is discovering new ideas. The world is constantly evolving with new inventions, thoughts, and philosophies. Staying open to new perspectives can broaden your understanding of life and challenge your beliefs.

That doesn't mean you have to agree with everything you hear, but being willing to listen and consider different viewpoints is crucial to growth.

Here are some ways to explore new ideas:

- **Expand Your Reading:** If you usually read one genre, try something different. Dive into topics outside your comfort zone.
- **Engage with Diverse People:** Talk to individuals with different backgrounds and experiences. Their perspectives may offer insights you haven't considered.

- **Attend Workshops**: Many community centers offer lectures or seminars on interesting subjects. It's a great way to explore new topics.
- **Follow Thought Leaders**: Use social media to follow diverse voices and thinkers, which can help expose you to fresh ideas.

By exploring new ideas, you strengthen your ability to think critically, question assumptions, and grow as a person.

Challenging Yourself to Improve

Growth often comes from pushing yourself outside of your comfort zone. When you challenge yourself, you discover abilities you didn't know you had.

Here are some ways to push your limits:

- **Set Learning Goals:** Choose a new skill you'd like to develop, break it into smaller steps, and work toward achieving it.
- **Face Your Fears:** Don't let fear stop you from trying new things. As I mentioned in my book, *Revisiting the Depths: Overcoming Fear and Finding Peace*, facing fears can lead to profound personal growth.
- **Embrace Mistakes:** Failure is part of learning. Mistakes teach valuable lessons and should be seen as opportunities to improve.

- **Seek Feedback:** Constructive criticism can be difficult to hear, but it's invaluable for growth.
- **Teach Others:** Sharing your knowledge with others not only helps them but reinforces your learning.

By continually challenging yourself, you expand your capabilities and open new paths for personal and professional success.

The Limits of Education

As important as education is, it's crucial to understand its limits. Education alone doesn't guarantee success; practical skills, emotional intelligence, and resilience are equally important.

While education can open doors, real-world experiences and a willingness to keep learning will ultimately determine your success.

Meaningful Insights:

- **Education is a Lifelong Journey:** Lifelong learning, through various experiences and self-directed exploration, is essential for personal growth.
- **Education as the Foundation for Growth:** Formal education provides the essential tools for critical thinking, problem-solving, and creativity, setting the foundation for lifelong learning and personal development.
- **Learning Beyond the Classroom:** Real-world experiences, hobbies, and travel can offer valuable lessons, complementing formal education by providing practical knowledge and insights.

12

Igniting Passion: A Journey Within

"People With Passion Can Change the World."

—Steve Jobs

P assion is that vibrant flame inside you—a deep interest that fills you with excitement and purpose. It's that magical feeling when time seems to vanish as you dive into an activity, lost in the joy of creation or connection.

For some, passion may flourish in creative outlets like writing, painting, or music, where every brushstroke or word holds a piece of their heart. For others, it may lie in helping people, serving the community, or tackling complex challenges that call for ingenuity and perseverance.

Finding your passion can feel like an exciting treasure hunt, full of moments of wonder and self-discovery. It's not just about uncovering what you love; it's about discovering what lights up your spirit and fuels your dreams. In a world that often feels chaotic and fast-paced, balancing passion with practicality can seem overwhelming. Yet, this journey is essential and transformative, guiding you toward a rich and fulfilling life.

The Power of Passion

Lessons from Trailblazers and Everyday Pursuits

There are countless examples of people driven by passion who achieved extraordinary success—Steve Jobs, Oprah Winfrey, and Jeff Bezos, to name a few.

As Oprah Winfrey once said, *"Passion is energy. Feel the power that comes from focusing on what excites you*[73]*."* These trailblazers advocate the importance of passion, coupled with hard work and perseverance, as essential for long-term success.

Steve Jobs believed, *"The only way to do great work is to love what you do*[74]*,"* while Jeff Bezos reminds us, *"In the world of business, the people who are most successful are those who are doing what they love*[75]*."*

Similarly, iconic historical figures such as Isaac Newton, Michelangelo, and Beethoven followed their passions in science, art, and music, leaving a lasting legacy.

While these famous figures may seem distant, their paths are not unique to those in today's spotlight. The principles they followed—passion, dedication, and perseverance—are accessible to everyone. Ask yourself: how does your passion connect with your deeper values and sense of identity? Does it reflect who you truly are, or perhaps who you aspire to become?

You don't need to be Steve Jobs or Oprah Winfrey to experience the fulfillment that comes from following your passion.

Whether your passion is in the arts, science, community work, or something deeply personal, the journey is the same: find what lights you up and pursue it relentlessly. The world may celebrate the famous for their achievements, but genuine success lies in the fulfillment you feel when you align your life with what brings you joy and purpose.

My Story on Passion

I have always had a deep passion for writing. In my journal, during my early twenties, I pictured a future where I would spend my days on the beach, lost in the rhythmic dance of words. To chase this dream, I boldly enrolled in a correspondence course with The Writer Bureau, a lucky find from a newspaper ad. However, life's changing priorities got in the way, and I never finished the course.

Years went by, and the dream lay dormant until a recent return to diving—an activity I hadn't pursued in thirty years—reignited my creative spark. It felt as if writing had been patiently waiting for me, calling out from deep within my soul. I thought about it constantly, jotting down my thoughts as soon as I woke each morning. That is passion—when it fills your every thought, pushing you forward with unstoppable energy.

As I poured my journey, emotions, and reflections into words, my book, *Revisiting the Depths: Overcoming Fear and*

Finding Peace—A Journey of Transformation, took shape. During the writing process, my only focus was on the authenticity of my journey. With each chapter I completed, I felt a deep sense of fulfillment and purpose, knowing I was staying true to my experiences and emotions.

Questions about its reception—Will it work? Will readers be moved? Will it sell?—hovered in the back of my mind but did not dominate my thoughts. Instead, I found comfort in knowing that somewhere, someone might find inspiration in my words.

This is the extraordinary power of passion and goal setting. It may take decades, but it works. A vision, when paired with strong goals, creates a roadmap that guides your actions and decisions. Even when the journey is tough and the path is unclear, these goals provide direction and purpose. Looking back on my life, I see how the dreams I recorded in a long-forgotten journal have come true. This serves as proof that patience, persistence, and unwavering faith can turn dreams into reality. Keep setting your goals and trust the process, knowing that your hard work will eventually pay off.

My son, I hope you find your passion in life. Discovering what drives you, what makes you feel alive and fulfilled, is one of the greatest gifts you can give yourself. Whether it's writing, music, art, science, or something else entirely, follow it with all your heart. Passion will help you navigate life's challenges, bringing joy and purpose to your days.

Practical Tips to Discovering and Pursuing What Truly Motivates You

- **Reflecting on What Motivates You:** To discover what truly motivates you, start by engaging in deep reflection about your interests. Think about the activities that bring you joy and make you lose track of time. What hobbies or subjects have always captivated you? Make a list of these interests to serve as a guiding light in your exploration. This list will be a treasure map, leading you toward the heart of your passion.

- **Leveraging Your Strengths:** Next, consider your strengths. What do you naturally excel at? Understanding your strengths can help you uncover your passions, revealing the unique ways you can contribute to the world. Pairing your strengths with your interests can create a stronger connection to your passion, giving you a sense of purpose that drives you forward.

- **Seeking Inspiration and New Experiences:** Inspiration often sparks passion, so actively seek out people and experiences that uplift you. Attend workshops that ignite your curiosity, read inspiring books that expand your horizons, or watch documentaries that resonate with your interests. These experiences can open doors to new ideas and motivate you to pursue what you truly love. Sometimes, finding your passion requires stepping beyond your comfort zone and embracing the unknown. This means trying new activities or hobbies that have always intrigued you. Whether it's joining a lively dance class, picking up a musical instrument, or volunteering for a cause close to your heart, these fresh experiences can uncover hidden passions and provide new perspectives that enrich your life.

- **Balancing Passion with Practicality:** Once you gain clarity about your passions, the next step is to find a delicate balance between following your heart and being practical. Yet, as inspiring as it is to pursue what you love, there's often a tension between the ideal vision of your passion and the demands of everyday life, like responsibilities and obligations. So, how do you reconcile this tension? How can you honor both your vision and your realities, blending passion with practicality in a way that supports your life and goals?

- **Creating a Plan for Success:** Having a thoughtful plan is essential for pursuing your passion while staying grounded in reality. Outline the steps you need to take to reach your goals, including time management, strategies, necessary resources, and a timeline for milestones. A structured plan can keep you focused and motivated, helping you navigate the inevitable ups and downs of the journey. Set aside dedicated time each week to focus on your passion, treating this time as sacred. This is your moment to reconnect with what you love and nourish your soul.

- **Building a Supportive Network:** Surround yourself with supportive people who understand your journey and share your aspirations. Whether it's friends, family, or a community of like-minded individuals, having a nurturing network can provide encouragement and accountability.

- **Celebrating Progress:** As you navigate toward your passion, take the time to celebrate the small victories along the way. Every step forward, no matter how small, deserves recognition and appreciation. Acknowledging these wins keeps your spirits high and reminds you that you are making tangible progress. Keeping a journal can be a powerful tool for self-reflection. Write down your thoughts, experiences, and feelings as you pursue your passion.

- **Infusing Joy into Your Pursuit:** Pursuing your passion should bring you genuine joy and fulfillment. While hard work is important, remember to infuse fun into your journey. Engage in activities that light you up and fill your heart with happiness. When you love what you do, the pursuit transforms into a rewarding adventure rather than a chore.

- **Integrating Passion into Your Career:** If possible, explore ways to weave your passion into your career. This doesn't always mean a job change; sometimes, it can mean shifting your focus within your current role to align better with your passions.

- **Overcoming Fear and Doubt:** Fear and doubt often linger when pursuing a passion. Recognizing your feelings is the first step toward overcoming them. Replace negative thoughts with uplifting affirmations. Positive self-talk nurtures confidence and empowers you to pursue your passion.

- **Visualizing Success and Developing Skills:** Visualization can be a powerful ally in this process. Picture yourself achieving your goals and living out your passion every day. This mental imagery can inspire you to take the necessary steps to turn your dreams into reality.

- **The Value of Mentorship:** Finding a mentor who shares your passion can be incredibly enriching and transformative. A mentor can offer guidance, support, and practical advice from their own experiences, helping you navigate the often rocky terrain of pursuing a passion.

The Pursuit of Passion

Finding your passion and pursuing it is an endeavor that takes time, patience, and unwavering effort. Welcome the process, celebrate your progress, and stay resilient in the face of challenges. Each step you take is a testament to your courage and commitment to living authentically.

Meaningful Insights:

- **Discovering Passion:** Finding your passion requires time, self-reflection, and openness to exploring what excites you and brings meaning to life.
- **Balancing Passion with Dedication:** Passion alone isn't enough; it takes hard work, persistence, and practical goal-setting to make your dreams a reality.
- **Living Passionately for Fulfillment:** Aligning with what you love brings purpose, joy, and a deeper sense of fulfillment, whether in work or personal life. It's about staying true to what genuinely matters to you.

13

Financial Wisdom for a Fulfilled Life

"A person can either discipline their finances or their finances disciplines them."

—Orrin Woodward

Money may not buy happiness, but it can bring freedom and peace. So, what does it take to build a wise financial life?

Financial wisdom involves making thoughtful, informed decisions about your money to create a secure and fulfilling life. It's not just about accumulating wealth but also about developing a healthy relationship with money—one that empowers you to achieve your goals without sacrificing peace of mind.

The quest for financial wisdom requires understanding, patience, and a commitment to continuous learning. In a fast-paced, consumer-driven society, it's easy to become overwhelmed by financial obligations, from managing daily expenses to planning for the future. By embracing financial wisdom, you can take control of your finances, prioritize what truly matters, and build a life that reflects your values and aspirations.

Living Within Your Means

At the heart of financial wisdom is the principle of living within your means. This simple yet powerful concept means spending less than you earn and making financial choices based on your current reality, not on societal pressures. In today's world, where advertisements and social media constantly promote the latest trends and luxuries, it's easy to get caught in the trap of overspending. The desire to keep up with friends or colleagues can lead to financial decisions that don't align with your long-term well-being.

Living beyond your means often results in debt, and the dangers of debt cannot be overstated. Credit cards, loans, and high-interest borrowing may offer short-term gratification, but they come at a steep long-term cost. When debt accumulates, it can feel like a heavy burden that's impossible to escape, leading to financial stress, anxiety, and a compromised quality of life.

To protect yourself from this cycle, it's important to cultivate habits of mindful spending, focusing on needs rather than wants and recognizing the true cost of impulse purchases.

Financial health starts with awareness. Ask yourself: Am I living within my means? Do I often spend money I don't have on things I don't truly need? By answering these questions honestly, you can begin to shift your mindset and make more intentional financial choices.

Prioritize Your Spending and Saving

Distinguishing between needs and wants is one of the most important steps toward financial wisdom. Needs are essentials—housing, food, healthcare—while wants are the extras that enhance life but aren't necessary for survival. This distinction becomes clearer when you take a moment to examine your spending habits. Are you prioritizing your needs over your wants? Are you making thoughtful, intentional decisions with your money, ensuring that each expense aligns with what truly matters to you?

Creating a budget is one of the most effective tools for staying on track. A budget helps you see exactly where your money is going, allowing you to identify areas of unnecessary spending and opportunities to save. Today, budgeting can be made easier with the help of apps or spreadsheets. The goal is to simplify the process, so it becomes a habit that you can sustain.

Saving is another critical component of financial wisdom, and it requires a mindset shift. Instead of viewing savings as something you'll do "later," make it a priority. Setting specific financial goals gives you a sense of purpose and motivation. Whether it's an emergency fund, a dream vacation, or long-term retirement savings, having clear targets helps you stay focused.

Small steps matter—don't feel discouraged if you can't save a large amount right away. Even modest contributions add up over time, and consistency is key. Consider setting up an automatic transfer to your savings account as soon as you receive your paycheck, turning saving into a habit rather than a chore.

Life is full of surprises, and having a financial safety net is essential for managing the unexpected. Experts recommend saving enough to cover six months' worth of living expenses in an emergency fund. Whether it's a medical emergency, a sudden home repair, or a job loss, this cushion provides peace of mind, allowing you to face life's challenges with confidence rather than fear.

Do you feel prepared for financial emergencies? If not, consider what small steps you could take today to build your emergency fund and strengthen your financial security.

Investing in Your Future

One of the most powerful ways to secure your financial future is through investing. Investing allows you to grow your wealth over time and make your money work for you. But financial wisdom in investing doesn't come from luck—it comes from education, research, and careful decision-making. If you're new to investing, start by educating yourself about how money works. There are countless resources available, from books to workshops to online courses, that can provide a solid foundation for understanding personal finance.

One highly recommended book for beginners is *Rich Dad Poor Dad* by Robert Kiyosaki[76], which outlines the differences between assets and liabilities and highlights the importance of financial literacy. Kiyosaki's approach offers practical insights into building wealth and making money work for you, although it's essential to critically evaluate and adapt his advice to fit your own financial circumstances.

Other valuable resources include Warren Buffett's Ground Rules by Jeremy C. Miller[77] and The Warren Buffett Way by Robert G. Hagstrom[78]. These books distill investment wisdom from one of the world's greatest investors, providing strategies for building wealth through careful, long-term investment.

While traditional investment advice remains relevant, the financial world is evolving rapidly. Today's discussions include digital assets like cryptocurrency, which come with higher levels of risk. Educating yourself on both traditional and modern investment strategies helps you make informed choices that align with your financial goals and risk tolerance.

Investment is not a one-size-fits-all process. Understanding your risk tolerance is crucial—some investments carry higher risks, but with the potential for greater rewards, while others are more stable but may yield lower returns. Start small, perhaps with low-cost index funds or savings accounts, and gradually expand your portfolio as you gain confidence and knowledge. Diversification is key to mitigating risk while maximizing potential gains.

Navigating Your Financial Journey

Financial wisdom is a journey that evolves over time. You will make mistakes along the way, and that's okay. Instead of allowing financial missteps to discourage you, view them as valuable lessons that can guide better decisions in the future. Financial challenges are inevitable, but how you respond to them makes all the difference.

Building a support system is another key element of financial success. Surround yourself with people who share similar values when it comes to money. Whether it's family members, friends, or a financial community, having people to talk to about your financial goals and challenges can be incredibly motivating. Open, honest conversations about money help reduce the stigma and isolation that sometimes accompany financial struggles.

Finally, embrace a mindset of gratitude and abundance. Instead of focusing on what you lack, take time to appreciate what you have. Celebrate your financial milestones, no matter how small. Each achievement is a step closer to your long-term goals, and maintaining a positive attitude can make the process much more enjoyable.

Lifelong Journey of Financial Wisdom

Financial wisdom is a lifelong journey that adapts as your life changes. There is no finish line—just continuous learning, growth, and refinement. By living within your means, budgeting effectively, saving diligently, and investing wisely, you can build a firm foundation for financial stability and security. With every decision you make, you are shaping your financial future.

If you ever feel overwhelmed, seek help from a professional. Financial advisors, coaches, or planners can offer personalized advice tailored to your unique situation, helping you develop a clear roadmap toward your financial goals.

The power to transform your financial life is within your hands. With patience, determination, and a commitment to learning, you can achieve financial wisdom and create the life you envision. Trust the process, stay focused on your goals, and let your financial wisdom guide you toward a secure, fulfilling, and abundant future.

Meaningful Insights:

- **Living Within Your Means Builds Financial Security:** Spending less than you earn is the foundation of financial peace. Avoid debt by making mindful spending and prioritizing financial stability.
- **Saving and Investing are Essential:** Prioritize saving consistently, even in small amounts, to build a financial safety net and achieve long-term goals. Educate yourself on investing to grow your wealth wisely.
- **Financial Wisdom is a Continuous Journey:** Financial success comes through continuous learning, adapting, and staying focused on your goals.

14

Prioritizing Health and Well-Being

"Take care of your body. It's the only place you have to live."

—Jim Rohn

66*...health is the wealth of wealth*[79]*.*" This quote by Richard Baker captures the concept that health is the foundation of all other forms of wealth, a reality often overlooked in our fast-paced, materialistic world.

Taking care of your health and well-being is one of the most valuable investments you can make in yourself. It goes beyond simply feeling good today; it lays the foundation for a better quality of life in the future. A healthy lifestyle encompasses making conscious choices that benefit your physical, mental, and emotional well-being.

Maintaining a Healthy Lifestyle

Imagine waking up every day feeling energized, with clear thoughts and a positive outlook. This is the power of maintaining a healthy lifestyle. Taking care of your body enables you to fully enjoy life, not just in the present, but well into the future. Picture yourself savoring the joy of playing with your kids or grandkids, exploring new destinations, or simply living without the burden of chronic pain or illness. These are the long-term benefits that come from making healthier choices today.

Nutrition: Fueling Your Body Right[80]

A cornerstone of good health is proper nutrition. The food you consume directly affects how you feel and function. It's not about adhering to strict diets or denying yourself the pleasures of food; it's about achieving balance and nourishing your body with a variety of foods. Incorporating more fruits, vegetables, whole grains, and lean proteins into your meals can make a significant difference. These foods provide essential nutrients that help your body function at its best, maintain a healthy weight, and protect against chronic diseases like diabetes, heart disease, and cancer.

Imagine sitting down to a vibrant salad filled with fresh vegetables, accompanied by a piece of grilled chicken and a slice of whole-grain bread. This isn't just a meal—it's a choice that actively supports your health. And you don't have to sacrifice your favorite treats. By practicing moderation and mindful eating, you can enjoy indulgences without guilt.

Exercise: Keeping Your Body Active and Strong[81]

Physical activity is equally vital. Regular exercise helps maintain a healthy weight, strengthens your muscles and bones, improves cardiovascular health, and elevates your mood. You don't need to spend hours at the gym to reap these benefits. The key is to find activities you enjoy and integrate them into your daily routine. Whether it's walking, cycling, dancing, or playing a sport, the important thing is to move your body consistently.

Picture yourself taking a brisk morning walk, the fresh air filling your lungs, and the rhythmic movement helping you clear your mind. Exercise doesn't have to be a chore—it can be a moment of peace and enjoyment. Or think about dancing to your favorite music, feeling the joy in your movements and releasing stress. Finding what you love will make staying active more sustainable.

Sleep: The Foundation of Rest and Recovery

Sleep rarely gets the attention it deserves, yet it's a crucial part of a healthy lifestyle. Quality sleep is necessary for your body to repair and regenerate, influencing your mood, memory, and overall well-being. Establishing a regular sleep schedule, creating a relaxing bedtime routine, and ensuring your sleep environment is comfortable can improve your sleep quality.

Visualize sinking into a cozy bed at the end of a long day, your mind and body ready to relax. The softness of the pillow, the warmth of the blanket, and the calm of the room create a sanctuary where you can let go of the day's stress. Good sleep prepares you to face the next day with energy and a positive attitude.

Staying Hydrated: The Power of Water[82]

Staying hydrated is another essential element of health. Water supports many vital functions in your body, including regulating body temperature, lubricating joints, and delivering nutrients to cells. Drinking enough water can enhance your sleep, cognition, and mood.

Picture the refreshing sensation of a cool glass of water on a hot day. It rejuvenates and revitalizes you. Making a habit of staying hydrated is one of the simplest yet most effective forms of self-care.

Listening to Your Body: Understanding Your Needs

It's important to listen to your body and respond to its needs. When you're tired, rest. When you're hungry, eat. If you're feeling overwhelmed, take a break. Your body gives you cue on what it needs—you just need to pay attention.

Think about the relief of stepping outside for a few moments to breathe when you're feeling stressed, or the satisfaction of a nutritious meal when you're hungry. These simple actions can make a profound difference in your health and well-being.

Self-Care: Prioritizing Your Well-Being

Balancing work and self-care are another critical aspect of health. In our busy lives, it's easy to get caught up in work and neglect our personal needs. However, self-care is not a luxury; it's a necessity. Taking time for yourself can enhance your productivity, prevent burnout, and improve your overall happiness.

Imagine the satisfaction of completing a work project knowing you performed at your best because you prioritized your health. Or envision the contentment of a restful weekend, where you recharged and pursued activities you enjoy. These moments of balance help maintain long-term well-being.

Surrounding Yourself with Positive Influences

Positive influences play a significant role in maintaining a healthy lifestyle. Surround yourself with people who encourage and inspire you. Engage in groups or communities that share similar interests and goals. A strong support system can make it easier to stay motivated and committed to your health.

Imagine the joy of sharing a nutritious meal with friends, the conversation and laughter enhancing the experience. Or the encouragement of a workout buddy who motivates you to keep going. These positive influences create a supportive environment that helps you thrive.

Creating a Healthy Home Environment

Your home environment plays a role in your well-being. A clean, organized, and peaceful living space can reduce stress and promote relaxation. Decluttering, using natural products, and incorporating elements of nature like plants can transform your home into a haven of health and well-being.

Picture walking into a tidy, well-organized home. Or imagine the tranquility of a room with fresh air, green plants, and natural light. These small changes make your home a sanctuary.

Healthy Lifestyle: Small Steps, Big Rewards

Maintaining your health is an ongoing pursuit. It's about making small, sustainable changes that add up over time. Being kind to yourself during setbacks is crucial. Every step forward, no matter how small, is progress.

Think about the pride in looking back at how far you've come—knowing your choices have supported your well-being.

The benefits of a healthy lifestyle go beyond feeling fit; they bring energy, joy, and the freedom to dive fully into the things you love.

Ultimately, living a healthy lifestyle means making choices that reflect your values and goals. It's a lifelong commitment to your physical, mental, and emotional health, and it's worth every step of the journey.

Meaningful Insights:

- **Invest in Your Health:** Prioritizing your well-being through balanced nutrition, regular exercise, quality sleep, and self-care sets the foundation for a fulfilling and vibrant life.
- **Listen to Your Body:** Your body gives you cue on what it needs—you just need to pay attention.
- **Small Steps, Big Impact:** Building a healthy lifestyle is about making small, consistent changes that align with your daily routine and long-term goals.

15

Mental Health Matters

---

*"I knew well enough that one could fracture one's legs
and arms and recover afterward, but I did not know that
you could fracture the brain in your head and recover
from that too."*

—Vincent Van Gogh

T he stigma surrounding mental health leaves many to
suffer in silence, yet it doesn't have to be this way. Mental
health struggles can feel like carrying an invisible weight,
pressing on every fiber of your being. Imagine a fog rolling in,
clouding your mind, making even the smallest choices seem
monumental. Some describe it as a tightrope walk, inching
forward with emotions and responsibilities balanced
precariously, all while concealing the truth from those closest to
them.

They wear smiles as if they're shields, hiding the hum of anxiety or sadness that lingers, dulling joy and dimming focus. This invisible battle runs deep, subtly shaping how they connect, work, and see themselves. When stigma keeps them silent, it only deepens the struggle, isolating them further in a fight that remains unseen.

Now, imagine waking up feeling at peace, handling stress without breaking down, and staying connected with the people around you. This isn't just a dream. By recognizing and addressing mental health challenges, building resilience, and developing effective coping strategies, it's within reach for everyone.

Recognizing and Addressing Mental Health Issues[83] [84]

We all face challenges in life. Sometimes these challenges can feel overwhelming, leading to feelings of sadness, anxiety, or even hopelessness. Signs of a deeper problem may include withdrawing from loved ones, losing interest in once-enjoyed activities, or constantly feeling sad. Acknowledging these feelings instead of brushing them aside is the first step toward healing.

Mental health issues often stem from a combination of internal and external factors. Internal factors include genetics, brain chemistry, early life experiences, and personality traits, all of which can contribute to an increased vulnerability to mental health challenges.

These internal factors shape how we interpret and respond to our environment, influencing resilience, self-esteem, and emotional stability. Thought patterns, such as chronic negativity and self-criticism, are internal contributors that may exacerbate mental health challenges.

External factors, such as trauma, social isolation, societal pressures, and lifestyle habits like sleep, diet, and screen time, also play a significant role in mental health. These influences often interact with internal factors, potentially amplifying challenges and disrupting emotional stability.

Recognizing these categories enables a holistic approach to mental health, acknowledging both the internal and external factors that shape well-being. By identifying the specific influences at play, you can develop targeted strategies to address and improve mental health effectively.

The "Pain Body" Unleashed

For Carmen, these challenges manifested in her everyday life. Gripping the steering wheel, her knuckles turning white as she edged forward in the slow crawl of morning traffic. The persistent buzz of her phone drew her eyes downward. She caught a glimpse of the email preview—a terse message from her boss, sent late the previous night. Her chest tightened as the weight of unspoken demands pressed down on her, a familiar wave of tension rising, engulfing her thoughts.

"Didn't meet expectations... could have been handled better."

A tight sigh escaped her lips as she let the phone drop back into its cradle. She barely had time to process the sting of those words before another notification lit up the screen, this time from her mother.

"If only you could find a stable job, Carmen. Think about it."

"Expectations," she muttered bitterly, her grip on the wheel tightening. "I'm doing my best, and it's never enough."

Her mind snapped back to reality as the sound of a car horn blared behind her. She pushed the accelerator as the light changed to green, her thoughts consumed by the email she had just read. Her boss's criticism intertwined with the constant sting of her mother's disapproval, leaving a lasting imprint on her emotions.

Just then, a black SUV veered in front of her, cutting her off and forcing her to brake hard. Her heart jolted as her coffee splashed over the rim of its cup, leaving a dark stain spreading across her skirt.

"Oh, come on!" she yelled, slapping her hand against the horn.

The driver in front threw up his hands in a quick, dismissive shrug, as if her frustration was nothing more than background noise, easily ignored.

"Right, just pretend I don't exist," she muttered, louder now. "Typical."

The passenger seat was empty, but she continued, words spilling out as if someone were there to listen. "Do they even care? Do they ever think about anyone else?" Her voice rose, raw with frustration that felt like it had been brewing for years. "Everyone thinks they can just push me around. Just like my boss, my mother, my sisters... like I'm invisible!"

A glance from the driver in the next lane caught her eye. He looked away, wide-eyed, and she turned to her reflection in the rearview mirror, noticing the tension etched into her face, the anger pulsing in her chest.

"What am I doing?" she whispered, her voice barely audible now, softened by a sudden, shaky realization. Her hand slipped from the horn, and she leaned back against the headrest, the weight of the morning sinking into her.

Around her, the hum of traffic receded into a muffled blur, as though she had stepped out of her life and into some muted silence. Her anger had flared so quickly, burning hot and fast, and yet... it didn't add up. She glanced down at her phone, at the unopened email waiting there, and felt a shift deep within.

This wasn't just about the traffic. It wasn't even about her boss or her mother's text. Beneath the surface, a simmering ache, rooted deeper than memory itself, was rising from somewhere long buried.

Carmen's story resonates, doesn't it? Her experience reflects a universal, often hidden, aspect of the human experience: the sudden eruptions of anger, frustration, or sadness that seem to come out of nowhere but are actually rooted in deeper, unresolved pain often without even realizing it.

Eckhart Tolle calls this the "pain body" in *The Power of Now*[85]. He describes it as an accumulation of past emotional pain lying dormant within us until something provokes it to life, causing us to react in ways that feel exaggerated or disproportionate. In these moments, our reactions are not only to the present but also to the echoes of past hurts, which resurface and intensify our feelings. Tolle explains that the pain body can take over our identity, consuming us until it "feeds" on emotions that match its energy: anger, grief, drama, even illness.

The Apostle Paul describes a similar inner conflict in Romans 7:17-24, King James Version, referring to the "flesh" as an aspect of ourselves that resists our better intentions. He writes, *"For what I want to do, I do not do, but what I hate, I do,"* capturing the frustration of feeling out of alignment with one's own desires and values. Like the pain body, Paul's "flesh" is a part of himself that acts against his conscious will, drawing him into a struggle between his higher self and his inner turmoil.

Psychologist Carl Jung also identified this phenomenon, calling it the "shadow[86]." The "shadow" represents those aspects of ourselves that we hide or deny, often because they don't align with our self-image or the values we wish to uphold. Yet, as Jung pointed out, these suppressed parts of us still influence our actions and emotions, sometimes in ways we don't recognize until they manifest as sudden outbursts or irrational reactions.

In Carmen's case, her "pain body", or "shadow", or "flesh"—is triggered by the pressures and disappointments of her daily life: her boss's disapproval, her mother's unmet expectations, and a stranger's dismissive gesture on the road. Each incident, minor on its own, taps into her stored feelings of invisibility and frustration, causing her emotions to overflow. Her anger isn't just about today; it's a release of years of feeling unseen and unheard.

When we recognize this pattern within ourselves, we gain an opportunity to confront these hidden parts. By acknowledging our "pain body" and bringing awareness to its presence, we create space for understanding and healing. Both Tolle and Jung emphasize that this courageous process dismantles the grip of unconscious forces, enabling us to reclaim inner peace, attain self-mastery, and embark on a transformative journey toward enduring personal growth.

How I Overcame My "Pain Body"

In my journey through life, the "pain body" has been an uninvited companion, slipping silently into my mind. These shadows crept in, coloring my reactions, guiding my decisions, and I felt them deeply, though I didn't fully understand their origins. Often, I reacted defensively, sometimes angrily, as though protecting something precious yet fragile within me. Yet the harder I tried to control these reactions, the more they seemed to control me, tightening their hold.

"I cannot let these negative feelings reign over me," I told myself one day, in a rare moment of clarity. "This is not who I am. This is not who I want to be. I don't want my loved ones to remember me this way."

But then I asked myself: Who am I? I am a reflection of the fruit of the Spirit, as discussed in *Chapter 4, Into the Light: Grounding in Faith*—love, joy, peace, forbearance, kindness, goodness, faithfulness, gentleness, and self-control. So, why am I not embracing these qualities? Why am I not allowing them to shape my life with purpose and grace?

Instead, I succumb to anxiety, worry, and stress—all manifestations of fear—fueled by my own imagined version of a hypothetical future. At the same time, I am weighed down by guilt, regret, resentment, defensiveness, bitterness,

188

unwillingness to forgive, and sorrow, each rooted in my past encounters. These emotions hold me captive, dictating my thoughts and actions, pulling me further away from the person I strive to be.

It was then that I recognized the "pain body" for what it was: not my true self, but a force grown from unprocessed hurt, fear, or insecurity, quietly shaping my life from the inside out. That day, I developed a way to recognize and manage this pain, starting with practicing self-awareness by nurturing the "observing ego"—a concept I introduced in *Chapter 1, Exploring Self: Beneath the Tip of the Iceberg*. I learned to step back, to witness the pain without becoming it. It begins by acknowledging the "pain body's" presence, meeting it as though it were an old friend who shows up unexpectedly, always uninvited, yet somehow familiar.

When these feelings rise—when the "pain body" stirs—I resist the urge to let it take over. I hold back, letting the sensations wash through me without allowing them to gain momentum. Often, in these moments, my heart feels heavy, as if it's bearing a weight I'm not sure I can carry. But I accept this heaviness, knowing that I am choosing to contain it, to hold it without letting it spill over to others.

And then, I release. Quietly, I surrender this energy to the Universe, which I call God. I offer these feelings, this burden, in silent prayer, asking for the strength to let go. In that act of release, the "pain body" loses its hold. The anger, the resentment, the hurt, the worry, the anxiety—they dissipate, like mist lifting off a lake in the early morning sun.

This isn't suppression; it's awareness—an honest acknowledgment of my emotions, a gentle letting go. I am no longer allowing the pain of my past or the worry of the future to steer me; I am learning to live beyond it, moving forward with clarity and peace.

Through this quiet practice, I am discovering the person I've always wanted to be beneath the pain: a person of grace, of compassion, a person who knows peace. And this journey, though ongoing, is uniquely mine, yet also universal—a testament to the resilience of the human spirit and the profound healing power of surrender. You, too, can develop this awareness, uncovering the strength within to live with purpose, clarity, and peace.

When I first began practicing the art of holding back my "pain body" and releasing it to the Universe, it wasn't easy. There were moments I stumbled, moments when my emotions flared despite my best efforts. I failed many times, and that's okay. This isn't a path of perfection, but one of persistence. Each attempt is a step forward, each misstep a lesson in patience, bringing us closer to peace.

With each practice, I learned to be gentler with myself. Every struggle became a step toward understanding, and gradually, my ability to release grew stronger. The "pain body's" grip loosened, bit by bit, allowing me to respond to life with more calm, compassion, and resilience. And as you continue on this path, you too will find the journey becomes lighter. Little by little, you will become aligned with the person you truly wish to be, and in that alignment, you will find peace.

Practical Tips for Mental Health

- **Seeking Support:** Talking about your feelings with someone you trust—whether a friend, family member, or therapist—is a powerful way to face mental health struggles. Professional help, such as therapy or counseling, can help you explore your thoughts and feelings, offer new perspectives, and guide you through difficult times.

- **Mindfulness and Self-Reflection:** Embrace the present moment fully, focusing on what's right now rather than what's missing. Journaling, meditation, and deep breathing help you observe emotions without letting them dominate your mind.

- **Surrendering and Letting Go:** When faced with emotional pain or your "pain body," begin by identifying the source of your feelings. Are they rooted in fear of an uncertain future or unresolved hurt from the past? Acknowledge these emotions without judgment, allowing yourself to sit with them rather than resist. As you recognize their origin, practice surrendering to the moment. Visualize these feelings as waves crashing and retreating on the shore—temporary, ever-changing, and incapable of holding you captive unless you cling to them. This conscious act of recognition and release helps dissolve emotional burdens and fosters inner peace.

- **Embrace the Spirit:** As you release these burdens, welcome the Spirit I spoke about earlier—the Spirit of love, joy, peace, forbearance, kindness, goodness, faithfulness, gentleness, and self-control. Let this Spirit fill the spaces left behind by fear and pain, shaping your life with purpose and grace. In embracing these qualities, you align yourself with a higher truth that nourishes your soul and guides you toward healing and wholeness.

- **Mindful Technology Use**: Social media can be helpful but also harmful. Limit your time if it affects your mood and instead focus on real-life connections. Be intentional with technology, setting boundaries such as turning off devices an hour before bed to reconnect with yourself and reduce stress.

- **Setting Boundaries**: It's okay to say no when you need to. Recognize your limits and prioritize your well-being. It's better to do a few things well than to spread yourself too thin.

- **Physical Well-Being:** Eating well, exercising, and getting enough sleep lay the foundation for good mental health. Joyful activities, such as spending time in nature or reading a good book, aren't indulgences but essential recharges. Carving out time for yourself reduces stress, improves mood, and helps you stay grounded, even in life's busiest moments.

- **Productivity and Goal-Setting:** Finding balance in work and life can prevent burnout. Setting priorities, breaking down overwhelming tasks, and focusing on one thing at a time helps make projects achievable and prevents stress from building. Clear goal-setting can also provide motivation and structure to keep you focused and fulfilled.

- **Managing Stress**: Coping strategies are the tools you use to manage stress and difficult emotions. Everyone's coping strategies differ; what works for one person might not work for another. The key is finding what works best for you.

- **Building Resilience**: Cultivate positive mindset to build resilience. It's not about never experiencing difficulties; it's about learning to recover from them.

- **Practice Self-Compassion:** Treating yourself kindly during hard times can help you cope and move forward with greater ease.

- **Practice Financial Wisdom:** Embrace the financial insights I shared in Chapter 13, *Financial Wisdom for a Fulfilled Life*. Let these principles guide your decisions, fostering a stable foundation for your future.

Mental Health as a Continuous Journey

Despite your best efforts, there may still be times when you struggle with your mental health, and that's okay. Everyone has bad days, and it's normal to feel down or anxious at times. When this happens, remind yourself that it's temporary and that you have the tools to navigate it.

Mental health is a pursuit that requires continuous attention and care. By recognizing and addressing mental health issues, building resilience, and developing coping strategies, you can lead a more balanced and fulfilling life.

Remember, you are stronger than you think, and you have the power to take control of your mental health. Reach out for help when needed, stay connected with loved ones, and prioritize time for yourself. Your mental health matters, and you deserve to feel good.

Meaningful Insights:

- **Prioritize Mental Health:** Recognize the signs of mental strain early and take proactive steps to address them.
- **Practical Tips for Mental Health:** Strategies include seeking support, practicing mindfulness, setting boundaries, and prioritizing physical well-being. Balance productivity with self-care, manage stress through personalized coping methods, and build resilience with a positive mindset and self-compassion.
- **Mental Health as a Journey:** Embrace mental health as a lifelong journey, viewing ups and downs as opportunities for growth and practicing self-compassion along the way.

16

Thriving Amid Change and Uncertainty

"Change is the law of life. And those who look only to the past or present are certain to miss the future."

—John F. Kennedy

Adapt or perish ...,[87]" a quote by H.G. Wells succinctly captures the idea that survival often depends on our ability to adapt to new circumstances—whether in nature, business, or personal growth. Change and uncertainty are as inevitable as the rising and setting of the sun. These forces shape our experiences, challenge our perspectives, and lead us down paths we never imagined.

Each transition, planned or unforeseen, offers a choice in how we respond. While comfort zones may feel safe, true growth lies in embracing the unknown. Developing a mindset rooted in resilience, adaptability, and self-discovery is not only a necessity but also a powerful tool. These qualities equip us to navigate life's highs and lows with confidence, grounded in the belief that we can handle whatever comes next.

The Path of Change

Imagine walking a familiar road, knowing every bend and curve. Suddenly, the path forks into an unknown direction. At first, this new route may seem intimidating, filled with uncertainty. However, it may also lead to exciting opportunities, fresh experiences, and even fulfillment you never expected. Embracing change is akin to stepping onto that new path with an open mind and a positive attitude. It means trusting yourself to navigate the unknown and understanding that challenges are stepping stones to growth.

The ability to adapt and remain resilient is essential in this journey. Think of a tree during a storm—the trees that bend with the wind are less likely to break than those that stand rigid. Similarly, when we embrace agility, we are better equipped to adjust our plans and expectations to fit new situations. This doesn't mean giving up on our goals; it means being open to new strategies and perspectives that help us reach them in ways we might not have fathomed. Could you approach future changes with a mindset that allows for growth and resilience, no matter where the path leads?

Change in Action: Real-Life Examples

From Consultant to Entrepreneur

I vividly recall the moment I stood at a career crossroads, feeling a mix of anticipation and fear. For years, I had envisioned a clear path to Partner—a journey where hard work and dedication would inevitably lead to success. That path felt stable, certain, like a well-trodden road lined with familiar markers of achievement. But life, as it often does, threw me a curveball. In a moment of clarity—or perhaps upheaval—I questioned everything I had worked toward.

That moment brought me back to a pivotal decision—to leave the corporate world and step into entrepreneurship. Walking away from a global consulting firm was more than just a career shift; it was an act of courage, driven by the desire to build something meaningful, something that truly resonated with who I wanted to become. Leaving meant facing not just professional uncertainty, but personal doubts I had buried for years.

My confidence, once a steadfast companion, wavered. Doubts crept in, subtle at first, then louder, relentlessly whispered in my mind: What if I made the wrong decision? What if I failed? What if, in leaving behind stability, I traded it for the sting of failure?

Fear of the unknown loomed large, casting a shadow over the future I had once taken for granted. I felt as though I were standing at the edge of a cliff, peering into an abyss, wondering if I would find solid ground—or plunge into the depths.

However, the idea of creating something for myself, of shaping not only my work but the impact it could have on others, was both exhilarating and terrifying. Embracing this change meant stepping into the unknown, a place filled with as much potential as it held uncertainty.

But as I stood there, confronting the abyss of the unknown, I realized that the path to growth was rarely clear-cut or predictable. Instead, it required a willingness to step forward despite the fear, trusting in the resilience I had cultivated over the years. It was never about surrendering control or embracing chaos. Rather, it was about trusting myself to navigate a path I couldn't fully see.

Embracing uncertainty and change became a powerful exercise in resilience and trust—trust in myself, in my vision, and in my ability to persevere through adversity. I saw obstacles not as barriers but as opportunities, each one a stepping stone toward the future I had yet to define. Rather than blocking my path, these challenges served as chances to learn, adapt, and grow.

From Singlehood to Marriage and Motherhood

Another significant change in my life was marriage. Suddenly, I was no longer just responsible for myself, but part of a larger, interconnected unit. When I married into a family with an only son, I realized the unique expectations that accompanied this role, especially in Asian families where traditions and family values are deeply held. Integrating into this new family came with its own set of challenges, as I adjusted to the rhythms, expectations, and long-standing customs of another household. It required patience, understanding, and resilience to find a balance between honoring my own values and embracing those of my partner's family. This dynamic shift felt both exhilarating and daunting as I navigated the complexities of combining our lives and families.

Then came motherhood—an experience more transformative than I ever imagined. Despite the countless pieces of advice and preparation, nothing could truly ready me for the moment I held my first child in my arms. It was overwhelming, humbling, and life-altering all at once. I remember feeling both awe and uncertainty, realizing that I was responsible for a new life, with no instruction manual in hand.

Motherhood quickly became a journey of discovery, filled with moments of joy and purpose that I had never experienced before. In learning to embrace change with grace, I found that motherhood pushed me to grow in ways I could never have foreseen, teaching me the profound value of resilience and adaptability with each new challenge.

Moving Countries: Navigating Cultural Shifts

Another pivotal change occurred when we moved across countries—from Kuala Lumpur to Makati, Bangkok, Jakarta, and eventually back to Kuala Lumpur. Each move was more than just a physical relocation; it involved leaving behind the support systems we had built and starting afresh. Uprooting wasn't just about moving to a new place; it was about leaving behind an entire ecosystem of friends, family, and community.

In Bangkok, the language barrier added another layer of complexity to our experience. While I had always been comfortable communicating in English, navigating daily life in a place where Thai was the primary language was challenging. Simple conversations required extra effort, and nuanced discussions often resulted in misunderstandings. There were moments of isolation and frustration. Yet, these challenges taught me the value of patience and the importance of finding alternative ways to connect. Whether it was learning a few key phrases in Thai, relying more on visual communication, or simply listening more attentively, I found new ways to bridge the gaps in understanding.

After years of living in Bangkok and adapting to its rhythm, returning to Kuala Lumpur was another significant change. Strangely, what was supposed to feel like coming home felt foreign. The long stay abroad had shifted our perspectives. For you, this transition was especially hard. Moving from a British school system to a local one in Kuala Lumpur was challenging—social dynamics, culture, and the education system were different, and it was a struggle to adapt. Witnessing this struggle in both of you was heartbreaking.

For me, the move meant leaving behind bonds I had nurtured in Bangkok. The friendships that had become a source of comfort were suddenly distant memories, and rebuilding those connections in Kuala Lumpur wasn't easy. Yet, through these challenges, I learned resilience, the power of community, and the importance of cultivating inner strength.

From Entrepreneurship to Corporate C-Suite

Life presented another major change when I transitioned from entrepreneurship to a corporate C-suite role. The change was drastic. After years of autonomy, I found myself accountable to a board, working within a team I didn't hand-pick, and navigating a corporate culture that often clashed with my own values. This required a mindset shift—learning to lead within an established framework while holding onto my principles.

Adapting quickly and decisively was critical. The role demanded new leadership skills, and the transition tested my ability to thrive amid changing circumstances. Although challenging, this experience reaffirmed my belief in the power of adaptability and resilience.

Reflection: The Power of Embracing Change

Embracing change and uncertainty isn't about merely enduring challenges; it's about thriving through them. Life often surprises us with the unexpected, but how we respond to these situations defines our future. Each challenge brings an opportunity to learn more about ourselves and the world.

Adaptability and resilience are essential. Just as a tree bends with the wind, we too must adapt to life's twists without breaking. Resilience grows with each challenge we face, and failure becomes a stepping stone to future success. Fear is a natural part of life, but it should not paralyze us. Instead, confronting our fears reveals our true strength and potential.

Support from others—family, friends, mentors—is crucial in this journey. Surrounding ourselves with positive, encouraging individuals strengthens our resolve. Their belief in our capabilities reinforces our confidence, helping us persevere through life's uncertainties.

Embracing change also means being open to new perspectives. Sometimes we become so attached to our ways of thinking that we overlook other possibilities. Openness fosters creativity and innovation, allowing us to continuously grow.

In our careers, adaptability is key. By embracing new skills, projects, and learning opportunities, we remain competitive. In personal life, trying new hobbies, meeting new people, or exploring new passions invigorates us, adding layers of fulfillment and joy to our journey.

Ultimately, embracing change with a positive mindset transforms how we approach life. We see challenges as opportunities for growth, failure as part of success, and the unknown as an exciting adventure. By cultivating resilience, adaptability, and perseverance, we can navigate life's uncertainties with confidence and grace.

Meaningful Insights:

- **Embrace Change for Growth:** Change and uncertainty are unavoidable, but seeing them as opportunities for growth and self-discovery can transform your perspective and build resilience.
- **Adaptability and Resilience Lead to Success:** Flexibility, like a tree bending in the wind, helps us navigate life's challenges. Resilience is strengthened through facing and overcoming obstacles.
- **Support and Openness are Key:** Surrounding yourself with a supportive network and staying open to new perspectives are essential for personal and professional growth, turning challenges into opportunities for success.

17

Discovering Life's Greater Meaning

"What lies behind you and what lies in front of you,
pales in comparison to what lies inside of you."

—Ralph Waldo Emerson

Discovering life's greater meaning is one of the most profound journeys we can undertake. This journey isn't merely about finding answers; it's about exploring questions that connect deeply to who we are. As we uncover our purpose, we begin to perceive the world in a new light. Our passions, values, and strengths intertwine, creating a profound harmony that guides our choices and actions. This process transforms our lives in ways we may never have anticipated.

Living with Purpose

Imagine waking up each day with a clear sense of why you're here. That clarity acts as a compass, guiding you through challenges and uncertainties. As Rick Warren explains in *The Purpose Driven Life*[88], *"You were made by God and for God, and until you understand that, life will never make sense."* Warren's approach to purpose emphasizes that true fulfillment comes from aligning our lives with a higher calling. It's not about self-centered pursuits but about understanding how our purpose contributes to something much larger than ourselves. Warren further states, *"You were put on this earth to make a contribution. You weren't created just to consume resources."*

When you see your purpose as a way to uplift and inspire others, you tap into a powerful source of motivation that propels you forward. This perspective shifts the focus from individual achievement to collective growth, creating lasting meaning in your actions.

When you live in alignment with your higher purpose— whether that's defined through spiritual understanding, personal values, or mindfulness—you experience life's deeper significance.

When you understand your purpose, decision-making becomes intuitive. Rather than feeling adrift, you develop a strong connection to your path. You know what to embrace and what to let go of. This newfound strength empowers you to face obstacles directly, recognizing each challenge as a stepping stone toward something greater.

Living with purpose brings a profound fulfillment, a deep satisfaction born from knowing you're a part of something larger. Whether through your work, relationships, or community, your actions reflect your core beliefs. Gradually, you see the ripple effects of your intentions—the positive impact you have on others and the world around you. This connection enriches your life and sparks a desire to inspire others on their journeys of discovery.

The Lifelong Process of Uncovering Purpose

As you journey through life, remember that discovering your purpose is not a single revelation, but a process that unfolds over time. It's a quiet, evolving journey, one that grows deeper with each experience. Like the protagonist in Paulo Coelho's *The Alchemist*[89], who finds meaning in both the challenges and triumphs along the way, your understanding of purpose will deepen over time. Purpose, like a tree, grows gradually—adapting, bending, reaching for the sky as it weathers each season. What once inspired you may shift as life brings new insights and paths. This gentle evolution, this flexibility, is part of life's beauty, allowing you to refine your purpose as you grow.

Sometimes, this journey will call you to step outside your comfort zone. Exploring new paths, meeting different people, or even exploring unexpected ideas can reveal facets of yourself you hadn't known. Embracing this openness allows your purpose to expand and mature, deepening your understanding of what truly resonates within you.

Another essential part of this journey is aligning your purpose with the values that silently shape your life. When your actions mirror what you genuinely believe, you create harmony and authenticity in your life. Imagine, for instance, if compassion or creativity is a value close to your heart.

Choosing a path that celebrates compassion—through acts of kindness, supportive relationships, or a career centered on helping others—reflects who you are. Or, if creativity guides you, finding outlets that allow for artistic expression, innovative thinking, or simply new ways to approach everyday life becomes fulfilling. This alignment between purpose and values brings joy that radiates outward, creating a steady integrity that others can sense and, perhaps, be inspired.

Overcoming Challenges and Celebrating Progress

Life's challenges often blur our sense of purpose, leaving us feeling as though everything is unraveling, causing us to question our path. Yet, these moments of struggle can also serve as powerful teachers, urging us to dig deep and uncover the resilience within. It is often through adversity that we come to realize what truly matters. For instance, someone who has faced illness might discover a renewed purpose in advocating for health awareness, transforming personal pain into a source of hope for others.

As you navigate this journey, remember to honor your progress. Each small step forward is a foundation upon which your purpose is built. Recognizing your achievements, however modest, can inspire you to keep going. Whether it's completing a project, offering kindness to someone in need, or simply reflecting on how far you've come, celebrating these moments nurtures a sense of fulfillment. This joy becomes the fuel that propels you forward, sustaining your journey of discovery and purpose.

Building Meaningful Connections

Finding your purpose isn't just about what you do; it's also about who you are becoming. It's a journey woven with the quiet, often profound connections you make along the way. Engaging with others allows you to see the world through fresh eyes, reminding you that you are part of something much larger. These connections might reveal paths you might not have considered, opening the way toward a deeper understanding of yourself and your role in the world.

When your life aligns with your purpose, you naturally draw close those who resonate with your vision, those who echo the beliefs that matter to you.

Imagine a circle of like-minded individuals who share in your passions, who uplift each other as you each strive toward dreams uniquely yours, yet intertwined. In this collective pursuit, purpose flourishes—a reminder that you are not walking this path alone but in harmony with others who light the way alongside you. In times of challenge, this community stands by you, offering perspectives that widen your own, inspiring you to keep moving forward.

Fostering a Deep Connection to the World

As you begin to understand your purpose, a quiet connection to the world around you may deepen. This sense of belonging brings with it a peaceful certainty, as though you're part of a larger story, weaving your unique thread into the fabric of life. In this realization lies a gentle strength, a reminder that even the smallest actions can ripple outward, creating meaning beyond what's immediately visible.

When you focus on what truly matters, the daily tasks and pressures of life soften, revealing moments of beauty and joy in the simplest things. Planting a tree, taking a stroll along the beach, or simply pausing to appreciate the changing seasons connects you to the earth's quiet wisdom. These moments with nature remind you that true fulfillment often comes from feeling part of something larger—an interconnected world that nurtures and sustains us all.

Embracing the Journey with Compassion and Mindfulness

As you walk this path, carry self-compassion as your quiet companion. The journey of uncovering your purpose is seldom smooth; it's marked by peaks and valleys, by seasons of clarity and moments of doubt. In those difficult times, remember to be kind to yourself. Kindness, especially to yourself, creates room for a clearer mind and an open heart, both of which you'll need as you move forward. This self-compassion becomes a wellspring of resilience, lifting you each time you stumble, helping you rise stronger with every setback life places in your way.

Embrace mindfulness as a powerful tool that draws you closer to your purpose, deepening your connection to the journey itself. This mindful presence invites you to pause, to reflect, and to savor each moment as it unfolds. As Eckhart Tolle emphasizes in *The Power of Now*, when we let go of fears about the future and regrets from the past, we free ourselves to embrace life more fully and connect with our true purpose in the present.

When you cultivate this awareness, you find clarity in unexpected places—a conversation, a quiet moment, or even within a challenge. These moments become gentle signposts, guiding you ever closer to the heart of your purpose.

Staying Open to Growth and Change

As you move forward, embrace a growth mindset—a willingness to see challenges as moments to learn, rather than walls that block your way. With this perspective, setbacks become less daunting, their edges softened by understanding.

Instead of fearing failure, you come to accept it as part of the journey. Each misstep holding a lesson that deepens your sense of purpose. In this way, resilience takes root, nurturing a strength that empowers you to keep going, even when the path ahead is uncertain.

Finding Joy in the Journey

As you move forward, welcome life's unpredictability with an open heart. The path to discovering your purpose is rarely straightforward. There will be twists, turns, and unexpected detours—moments that may feel like setbacks but are, in truth, threads woven into the fabric of your growth. Welcoming these experiences with openness allows you to adapt, to deepen, and to witness life in all its intricate layers. Each encounter, each bend in the road, each twist, and each detour adds richness to your understanding of what it means to live with purpose.

In the end, finding your purpose is about embracing life's beauty in all its complexity. It's about discovering joy not only in the outcome but in every step along the way. As you explore, grow, and connect, you begin to craft a life that feels whole, imbued with meaning and fulfillment. This journey is yours alone—a unique adventure, with each step drawing you closer to the greater purpose that resides within.

So, as you continue on this path, remember to stay grounded in your values, savor the process, and celebrate each discovery. Your purpose is a beacon, guiding you through the vast and wonderful landscape of life, illuminating the way to a future filled with meaning and joy.

Meaningful Insights:

- **Purpose is a Lifelong Journey:** Discovering your purpose is an ongoing process of growth and self-reflection. It evolves as you face new challenges and opportunities, guiding your life toward greater meaning.
- **Mindfulness and Self-Compassion are Key:** Being present in the moment and practicing self-compassion through life's ups and downs helps you stay connected to your purpose. Mindfulness allows you to embrace opportunities, while self-compassion builds resilience during challenges.

- **Purpose is About Contribution:** True fulfillment comes from aligning your life with your values and contributing to something larger than yourself.

18

A Mother's Love and Legacy

The story of my mother's legacy wasn't recorded in grand gestures or written in words, but in the quiet strength she carried, even when her world shattered.

Have you ever thought about the story you're crafting in your life? Every choice, every relationship, every challenge, every encounter—it all adds up to the narrative that defines who you are and how others experience you. It's not about the titles or possessions we collect—it's about the lasting imprint we leave on the hearts and minds of others. Your story isn't written in a single, grand moment. It's built in the everyday decisions, the small actions, and the way you engage with the world.

Each of us carries a unique story, and that story shapes how we navigate our lives and connect with others. This is your story—it's time to live it with intention.

My Mother's Sorrow

Losing the Love of Her Life

When my father passed away, my mother was left to navigate the stormy seas of grief, her once-steady ship now adrift in a violent storm. The winds of grief tore through her sails. The anchor of her life—the love of my father—was gone. She drifted in an ocean of sorrow. Each wave threatened to pull her under, but somehow, she stayed afloat, weathering a storm no one else could see.

Losing her soulmate left a void that felt bottomless, an emptiness that seemed impossible to fill. Her sorrow became a palpable presence, entwining itself into every part of our daily lives. The air in our home felt heavy with sadness, each breath a reminder of the absence that had shattered our world.

My mother, already a pillar of strength, now faced the overwhelming task of raising three young children alone. The weight of this responsibility pressed down on her, yet she bore it with quiet dignity and determination.

In those early days, her every action was marked by grief, but there were still small glimpses of strength. She clung to routine—ensuring we attended school on time, preparing meals, and keeping the house in order as though she were holding together the fragile threads of our fractured lives.

Her sorrow was intense, a deep and unending ache, but she rarely allowed it to show. Instead, she channeled her grief into ensuring that we felt safe, loved, and supported.

One way she expressed this was through the meals she prepared—not just typical dishes, but meals specifically crafted for each of us. For me, there were days when she'd steam a white pomfret with ginger and soy. My elder brother would sometimes find himself greeted with roasted "siew yoke" (pork), its skin crackling with perfection and the aroma of five-spice and tradition. For my youngest brother, it was prawns in tomato gravy, simmered gently until tender, the rich sauce coating every bite. It was more than just nourishment; it was her way of silently saying, "I see you, I know what comforts you, and even in my grief, I am here for you."

Each plate was a reflection of her enduring love, a way of holding us close when words often failed, even as her heart was breaking.

There were moments, though, when the façade of strength would crack, revealing the raw pain beneath. Late at night, when she thought we were asleep, I would hear her soft sobs—the sound of a heart breaking anew each night. In those quiet hours, she would sit by the window, gazing out into the darkness, her tears mingling with whispered words of longing and love.

These moments of vulnerability only deepened her resilience. Even in her pain, she seemed instinctively aware of ours, offering quiet reassurance without words—a gentle touch on the shoulder, a knowing glance, a soft smile. Her love became our refuge, her quiet acts of comfort a lifeline as we navigated the dark waters of our shared loss.

Her sorrow was not just for the love she had lost, but also for the future they had dreamed of together. The plans and hopes they had nurtured now lay in ruins, leaving her to forge a new path alone. She mourned not only for herself but for the family left incomplete, the father her children would now grow up without.

As the months passed, I noticed the subtle ways she rebuilt herself. Beneath her grief was a quiet determination, an emerging resilience that manifested in her ability to care for us despite the weight of her sorrow.

Despite her grief, my mother never allowed herself to be consumed by it. One moment stands out: months later, I saw her laugh again. It was brief, fragile, but in that fleeting moment, I saw the beginnings of her reclaiming joy, her spirit flickering back to life.

In the years that followed, her sorrow remained a constant companion, a shadow that never fully disappeared. Yet, she also found moments of joy and laughter—small victories that reminded her, and us, of life's beauty, even amidst pain. This marked a turning point where her sorrow, though ever-present, coexisted with moments of light.

Her character evolved as she learned to live with her grief, not as something that consumed her but as a companion that ultimately became a source of strength. Each small victory, each laugh, and each quiet act of love deepened the bond between us, despite the tremendous weight of loss she carried.

My mother's sorrow, born from the premature loss of her soulmate, shaped her into a remarkable woman. It taught her—and us—that even in the face of unimaginable pain; it is possible to find a way forward. Her journey through grief was a testament to the enduring power of love and the unbreakable bond of family.

My Mother's Battle with Cancer
A Journey of Hope, Pain, and Love

In mid-1997, everything changed. My mother, my anchor, my confidante, was diagnosed with stage 4 cancer. It hit us like a sledgehammer, shaking the foundation of our lives. I remember her hands trembling, though her voice remained steady as she reassured us. Beneath that calm exterior, I saw a vulnerability I had only witnessed once before—when my father passed away.

My mother had always been the epitome of grace— gentle, forgiving, and endlessly compassionate. She had a remarkable ability to hide her pain, always putting us first. But now, I could see the quiet battles she fought, not just against the cancer, but against her own fears. Fear of the future, fear of leaving us, and fear of her own mortality.

Despite the bleak prognosis, we rallied together, determined to fight this beast with every ounce of strength and hope we could muster. We embarked on a grueling journey, beginning with chemotherapy. Each session was a test of endurance, not just for my mother but for all of us who watched helplessly as the treatment drained her vibrant energy. The nausea, hair loss, and relentless fatigue were brutal, yet she faced it all with unwavering courage.

There were days when the pain was etched in her face, but her eyes always held onto hope. Her resilience became our beacon, and we clung to the belief that this was a fight we could win.

Months later, we moved to radiotherapy, clinging to the hope that this would bring a miracle. But fate dealt us a cruel hand. Instead of shrinking, the cancer spread with a vengeance, infiltrating other parts of her body. It was a devastating blow, shattering the fragile hope we had built. I could see it in her eyes, though she tried to mask it—hope slipping away, piece by piece.

Letting Go with Grace

The evening news droned in the background as I sat beside her, her frail hand cool in mine. She turned her head slowly, meeting my gaze with a soft, familiar smile—a smile that, even in her weakened state, still carried warmth. "It's okay," she whispered, her breath barely audible. "I'm ready to go."

Her words lingered between us, heavy with finality but infused with a quiet peace. My heart clenched, and for a moment, I couldn't speak. Tears welled up in my eyes as I searched her face, looking for any trace of fear or doubt—but there was none—just an acceptance that wrapped itself around her like a gentle cloak. It wasn't surrender; it was a transition.

I tightened my grip on her hand, not wanting to let her go, even though I knew I had to. "Mom," I choked out, "I don't know how to do this without you."

She gave me the smallest of smiles, her lips barely curling, but it was filled with the love and reassurance only a mother could give. "You already know how. You've always known."

In that moment, I realized she wasn't holding onto life any longer. She wasn't clinging to what she was leaving behind. Instead, she was preparing me for the world without her, offering comfort in the only way she knew how. Her words were filled with the weight of a mother's love—selfless, brave, focused not on her suffering, but on easing mine.

She was letting go, not because she had lost the fight, but because she had found her peace. And in that quiet surrender, she taught me one final lesson: that sometimes true strength lies in letting go, and courage is in accepting the things we cannot change.

I squeezed her hand, fighting the lump rising in my throat. A quiet strength radiated from her, as if, even now, she was the one holding me together.

Her gaze flicked briefly to the corner of the room, the faintest smile tugging at her lips. "When it's time," she said, almost as if she were discussing plans for a small family dinner, "I want to be cremated. Simple. No fuss."

She looked at me, her eyes steady, as if to reassure me that this was how she truly wanted it—modest, like the life she had lived. "No elaborate casket," she added, her fingers twitching lightly, dismissing any notion of extravagance. "Something plain."

She fell quiet for a moment, her eyes distant, as if searching through memories. "The pearls..." she murmured, so softly it was as though she were speaking to herself. I didn't need to ask which ones—she meant the necklace tucked away in the old wooden box, a gift she treasured but wore only on special occasions. "I'd like to wear them... on that day."

Her fingers traced the armrest of her chair, each word deliberate, full of thought. "And the dress..." she added, her voice trailing off. A faint smile tugged at her lips, and in that

224

instant, I knew which dress she meant—the one she wore on my wedding day. "That was one of the happiest days of my life," she said softly, her eyes reflecting the joy of that memory.

That dress, still filled with the life and laughter of that day, had become a part of her story. She wanted to leave wrapped in the memory of love and family, a celebration that had filled her heart. The flicker in her eyes told me the laughter and love of that day were still alive in her.

Her gaze softened as it rested on the leather brown shoes by the door—the ones I had bought for her during my last week as an undergraduate in Australia. She looked at them for a moment, her expression tender. "And those shoes," she whispered, her voice carrying the weight of distance, of the bond that had bridged the miles between us.

Each item she chose held a memory, a connection, and in her quiet way, she was weaving our shared history into her final farewell. She envisioned everything with simplicity, as if to say that even in her passing, she wanted to leave us with the essence of who she truly was—humble, loving, and full of heart.

She had thought through every detail carefully, with love and consideration—not for herself, but for us. Each choice eased our pain, to ensure that we wouldn't be burdened by extravagant gestures or difficult decisions. Her final act of love was to lighten our grief by removing the weight of uncertainty, offering us the comfort of knowing we would honor her wishes exactly as she wanted.

Fading Between Worlds

As the cancer advanced, my mother's pain became unbearable. The doctors prescribed heavy doses of morphine, but the relief it provided was fleeting. The agony was relentless, and it broke my heart to see her suffer.

The morphine brought with it a haze of hallucinations, pulling her in and out of reality. She would speak to people who weren't there, reliving fragments of the past with a mix of clarity and confusion.

In those final days, I stayed by her side as much as I could. Her body, once full of life, was now a delicate shell. Every breath seemed like an enormous effort. The nights were long and filled with a suffocating mix of fear and sadness. I held her hand, whispered words of love, and tried to ease her pain. Each moment was a precious gift, yet also a painful reminder of the inevitable.

After she passed, the emptiness was unbearable. The house felt hollow, her absence a void that nothing could fill. Grief came in waves, each one more overwhelming than the last. But amid the sorrow, there was also gratitude—for the time we had, for the love she gave, and for the chance to be with her until the end. Her love became the guiding light in the darkness of my grief.

Decades have passed, and whenever I revisit this chapter of my life, it is as if time has never moved on. The pain remains excruciating, a stark reminder that time does not heal all wounds—it only teaches us to live with them.

But her spirit endures. In the way I live my life, in the love I share with others, and in the quiet moments of reflection, I still feel her presence. Her strength, her grace, and her love continue to guide me, just as they did when she was here. And though she is no longer with me, her memory is a constant reminder of the profound impact one life can have on another.

A Testament to Love and Strength

My mother's love and strength weren't qualities she possessed—they were the essence of everything she did. Her legacy wasn't in the things she said, but in the life she lived, and in the countless ways she touched those around her.

Her legacy is a rich canvas painted with strokes of grace, kindness, and unwavering love. Every act, no matter how small, was an expression of her boundless compassion. She taught me that courage is not the absence of fear but the strength to press forward despite it.

Even in the face of unimaginable pain, my mother showed resilience that transcended her suffering. In her final days, despite the toll of cancer, she never let her spirit dim. She smiled in moments of agony, offering comfort when it was her who needed it most. It's this quiet grace, this ability to hold on to joy even as she faced death, that left the deepest mark on my life.

Her unconditional love became the foundation upon which I continue to build my life. In moments of uncertainty, when I feel overwhelmed by the weight of the world, I hear her voice—a soft yet steady reminder to stay true to my values and treat others with the kindness she embodied.

As I reflect on my mother's life, I'm reminded of the legacy I hope to leave—a legacy that mirrors the love and strength she exemplified. Her spirit lives on, a beacon of light guiding those she touched through life's challenges. Her legacy is a powerful reminder of the impact one person can have.

Though her time was cut short, her influence continues to illuminate my path, reminding me that while life may be unkind, love is the force that carries us through. It is the light that shines in the darkest times.

Thinking about the life she had lived, I can't help but wonder—what story will you write with your life? Like my mother, you too have the power to leave a legacy of love, strength, and kindness—one that will echo in the hearts of those you touch.

The choices you make today are the building blocks of that legacy—make them with intention, with love, and with purpose.

Meaningful Insights:

- **Legacy is Built in Small Acts:** Your everyday choices of love, kindness, and strength shape the legacy you leave behind.
- **Resilience Defines You**: True strength is revealed in how you rise through adversity, finding grace even in difficult times.
- **Live with Purpose:** Every decision you make today shapes the legacy that will live on in the lives you touch.

Conclusion: A Journey Together

Son,

As you stand on the brink of new beginnings, I hope this book has provided you with guidance, wisdom, and direction from the deepest parts of my heart. Writing these chapters has been a labor of love, a way to share the life lessons I've gathered on my journey with you as you carve your own path.

We've explored the importance of staying connected to your faith, nurturing personal growth, and cherishing friendships and relationships. We've delved into building meaningful connections, upholding solid ethical and moral principles, and embracing challenges with resilience. These lessons form the foundation of a life filled with purpose, fulfillment, and joy.

As you move forward, remember that life is a series of transitions, each offering its own opportunities for growth and self-discovery. From your days as a student to becoming a professional, from being single to finding a life partner, and eventually stepping into parenthood, every stage of your life adds a unique thread to your existence.

In your career, whether you're climbing the corporate ladder or embarking on an entrepreneurial journey, both paths will require you to embrace leadership roles and navigate obstacles with integrity and tenacity.

Stay humble and grateful for the blessings you receive, and always maintain a positive outlook, even when faced with difficulties. Set goals and prioritize your aspirations, knowing they are the roadmap to your success. Embrace lifelong learning, for knowledge continually enriches your life.

Pursue your passions with unwavering dedication. Financial wisdom is essential for a stable and fulfilling life, so manage your resources wisely. Take care of your health and well-being, both physical and mental, for they are the foundations of a vibrant life. Seek life's greater meaning, understanding that true fulfilment comes from living in alignment with your values.

Yesterday is history, today is a gift, and tomorrow is a possibility. This timeless wisdom reminds us to live our lives to the fullest—love deeply, laugh often, and embrace every moment with gratitude and joy. Be kind to yourself, and never let the past define you.

As you read this final chapter, know that my heart is always with you, celebrating your victories, offering comfort in times of need, and cheering you on every step of the way. The life lessons I've shared are more than just words; they are expressions of the love and hope I have for your future.

Remember, my son, that leaving a legacy is not just about the wealth you accumulate but the impact you have on others, the kindness you show, and the love you spread. Your journey is uniquely yours to shape, and I have every confidence that with your faith, wisdom, strength, and compassion, you will create a life that is both successful and deeply meaningful.

As you turn the page to your next chapter, remember that you are never alone. Our bond transcends time and space.

Walk your path with faith, courage, and an open heart.

APPENDIX

4-QUADRANTS PERSONAL GROWTH MODEL

Throughout this book, I've shared stories and insights to inspire you to navigate life with courage, purpose, and grace. As we bring this journey to a close, I want to leave you with a tool for lasting personal growth—a framework to nurture every facet of your being.

I call it the **4-Quadrants Personal Growth Model**, a holistic approach that embraces the harmony we all seek: growth that enriches your spirit, sharpens your mind, empowers your work, strengthens your financial foundation, and deepens your relationships.

Developed from the lessons explored in this book, this model isn't a set of rigid rules. It's a compass—a gentle guide to help you live with greater intention, balance, and fulfilment.

1. Spiritual Growth

Focus: Cultivating inner peace, self-awareness, and alignment with your values.

In a world filled with noise, spiritual growth is the quiet work of coming home to yourself. It's about finding moments of stillness and grounding yourself in what truly matters.

Examples to Try:

- **Daily Meditation / Prayers:** Begin and end your day with 10–15 minutes of mindfulness meditation or prayers to center yourself, set intentions, and reflect with gratitude.

- **Nature Walks:** Spend time in nature, observing its beauty, connecting with the natural world, and appreciating the environment that sustains us.
- **Journaling**: Write about your thoughts, feelings, and experiences to gain self-awareness.
- **Developing the Observing Ego:** Cultivate the ability to step back and witness your thoughts, emotions, and reactions without judgment.

How You'll Know You're Growing:

You might notice the weight of stress lifting. There's a sense of calm and peace, even in chaos, and your choices feel more aligned with your values. Growth here is subtle but powerful, like a seed growing underground before it breaks through the soil.

2. Social Growth

Focus: Deepening connections with others while nurturing physical and mental well-being.

At the heart of social growth is relationship—our relationship with ourselves, with loved ones, and with the communities we belong to. This quadrant reminds us we're not alone, and that life is richer when shared.

Examples to Try:

- **Schedule Social Time**: Set aside dedicated time for meaningful social interactions, whether it's a weekly coffee date with a friend, family dinner, or even a casual call to reconnect with someone important to you.

- **Practice Deep Listening:** Engage fully with those you speak to by practicing deep listening. Ask open-ended questions to encourage authentic exchanges and deeper emotional connections.

- **Join a Community:** Participate in clubs, groups, or volunteer organizations that resonate with your passions and interests, creating opportunities to connect with like-minded individuals.

- **Nurture Self-Care:** Prioritize activities that rejuvenate your physical and mental well-being, such as exercise, relaxation techniques, or hobbies that bring you joy.

- **Learn to Identify and Release Your Pain Body:** Recognize recurring negative emotions or thought patterns that weigh you down emotionally. Work on releasing these patterns through mindfulness, self-awareness, or therapeutic practices to free yourself from emotional reactivity and cultivate inner peace.

How You'll Know You're Growing:

Your relationships will feel deeper, not because you spend more time together, but because you connect more meaningfully. You'll notice your body and mind becoming revitalized, giving you the energy, clarity, and peace to embrace life and all its demands.

3. Intellectual Growth

Focus: Expanding your knowledge, creativity, and problem-solving abilities.

Intellectual growth isn't just about acquiring facts—it's about curiosity. It's that spark of wanting to know more, understand deeper, and express yourself in ways you never thought possible.

Examples to Try:

- **Lifelong Learning**: Invest in personal growth by reading widely, taking online courses, and attending workshops or conferences that broaden your knowledge and skills.
- **Cultivate Creativity**: Explore creative outlets like journaling, painting, or playing an instrument to nurture self-expression and innovative thinking.

- **Critical Thinking**: Develop a curious mindset by questioning assumptions, analyzing information critically, and engaging in meaningful debates or discussions.

How You'll Know You're Growing:

You'll find yourself inspired—by an idea, a skill, or even a mistake that taught you something valuable. Intellectual growth is not about being perfect; it's about being engaged, awake, and open to learning.

4. Financial Growth

Focus: Building a meaningful career or venture while cultivating financial stability.

This quadrant isn't just about ambition—it's about purpose. It's about creating work that aligns with who you are, while also building a foundation for financial stability and paving the way toward long-term financial freedom.

Examples to Try:

- **Financial Planning:** Create a budget to monitor income and expenses, set financial goals, and consult a financial advisor for a personalized plan.

- **Career Development:** Identify your strengths, network with industry professionals, and commit to continuous learning to enhance your career.
- **Investing:** Start investing early to benefit from compound interest, diversify your investments to mitigate risk, and seek professional advice for informed decisions.
- **Side Hustles and Entrepreneurship:** Leverage your skills or passions to generate additional income.
- **Wealth Management:** Learn about taxes, savings plans, and long-term financial security to ensure you are optimizing your resources for future growth.

How You'll Know You're Growing:

Growth in this quadrant is measured in tangible economic outcomes. It might look like an increased income, achieving a financial milestone like purchasing a home, or diversifying your income streams through investments or a side hustle. Beyond these outcomes, it's also about developing confidence in your ability to manage finances and make sound economic decisions.

A Framework for Life

The **4-Quadrants Personal Growth Mode**l is not meant to be a checklist. Life is unpredictable, and growth is never linear. There will be days when you feel you've mastered one quadrant and days when you feel you're starting over in all four. That's okay.

Growth is not about perfection—it's about presence. It's about showing up for yourself and the people you love, day after day, even when it's hard.

As you reflect on this model, remember that spiritual growth serves as the foundation, grounding and guiding all other areas of your life. The inner peace and clarity you cultivate spiritually can enhance intellectual focus, inspire meaningful social connections, and provide the strength to pursue your career with purpose. Each quadrant feeds into the others, creating a harmonious balance where growth in one area naturally supports and enriches the rest. This model is not the destination—it's your personal growth expedition. And I hope it leads you to a life that feels whole, balanced, and deeply yours.

ACKNOWLEDGEMENT

Writing this book has been an incredible process, and I thank God for providing me with the strength, inspiration, and perseverance to complete it.

I am deeply grateful to those who have supported me along the way:

To my husband, Eugene, your support and love have been invaluable. Thank you for encouraging and believing in me.

To my children, Emily and Daniel, your love and patience have been my greatest source of strength.

To the talented team behind this book and audiobook—editor, formatter, book cover designer, marketing consultant, audiobook narrator, and producer—your collective dedication and expertise have been invaluable. Thank you for your hard work and commitment to bringing this project to life.

To my readers, thank you for embarking on this journey with me. Your support means the world to me.

ABOUT THE AUTHOR

Amy Tan is an accomplished business executive and award-winning author with over twenty years of experience in corporate leadership and market expansion across Southeast Asia. She holds a Business Administration degree from the Royal Melbourne Institute of Technology and a Postgraduate Certificate from the University of Nottingham.

Beyond her corporate role, Amy is a passionate storyteller, weaving her diverse experiences into narratives that explore personal growth, resilience, and transformation. Her recent book, *Revisiting the Depths - Overcoming Fear and Finding Peace,* which won the Literary Titan Gold Book Award, recounts her emotional and spiritual journey as she overcomes a long-held fear of the ocean through diving.

Amy's latest book, *Life Lessons from Mom: For the Man You'll Become,* is a thoughtfully crafted guide that offers practical wisdom on navigating life's challenges, cultivating meaningful relationships, and building a legacy of love. She is also the author of *Doing Business in ASEAN* and *China: An Ultimate Guide to Doing Business,* which showcases her expertise in regional economic integration.

Having lived in Malaysia, Thailand, the Philippines, and Indonesia, Amy brings a rich, cross-cultural perspective to her writing, inspiring readers to overcome challenges and make positive changes. Her work highlights the powerful impact of storytelling on personal and professional development.

NOTES

Chapter 1

[1] Edwards, J. (2024, October 15). *Bitcoin's Price History*. Investopedia. https://www.investopedia.com/articles/forex/121815/bitcoins-price-history.asp

[2] Maor, D., Kaas, H.-W., Strovink, K., & Srinivasan, R. (2024, June). *The 'Inside Out' Leadership Journey: How Personal Growth Creates the Path to Success*. McKinsey & Company. https://www.mckinsey.com/capabilities/people-and-organizational-performancc/our-insights/the-inside-out-leadership-journey-how-personal-growth-creates-the-path-to-success

[3] Peck, M. S. (2003). *The Road Less Traveled: A New Psychology of Love, Traditional Values, and Spiritual Growth*. Touchstone

[4] Jung, C. (n.d.). *Who Looks Outside, Dreams; Who Looks Inside, Awakes*. BrainyQuote. https://www.brainyquote.com/quotes/carl_jung_132738

[5] Tolle, E. (1999). *The Power of Now*: *A Guide to Spiritual Enlightenment*. New World Library.

[6] Cleveland Clinic. (2023, ay 2). *Cognitive Bias 101: What It Is and How To Overcome It*. https://health.clevelandclinic.org/cognitive-bias

[7] Tan, A. (2024). *Revisiting the Depths: Overcoming Fear and Finding Peace - A Journey of Transformation*. Books to Hook Publishing, LLC

Chapter 2

[8] R. Crisp, Trans. (2014). *Aristotle: Nicomachean Ethics*. Cambridge University Press. (Book VIII, Section 3).

[9] Winfrey, O. [Oprah Winfrey]. (2020, April 15). *Oprah Winfrey Talks to Thich Nhat Hanh About Deep Listening* [Video]. YouTube. https://www.youtube.com/watch?v=CywxW1ImPCQ

[10] Villines, Z. (2024, January 31). *What to Know About Malignant Narcissism*. Medical News Today. https://www.medicalnewstoday.com/articles/malignant-narcissist

Chapter 3

[11] Austin, D. (2024, February 9). *What Happens to Your Body When You're in Love—and When You're Heartbroken*. National Geographic. https://www.nationalgeographic.com/premium/article/love-loss-death-hormones-brain-heart-health

[12] Gray, J. (1992). *Men are From Mars, Women are From Venus: A Practical Guide for Improving Communication and Getting What You Want in Your Relationships*. HarperCollins

[13] Peck, M. S. (1998). *The Different Drum: Community Making and Peace*. Touchstone

Chapter 4

[14] Coe, E., Enomoto, K., Brassey, J., & Bennett, V. (2024, May 13*). In Search of Self and Something Bigger: A Spiritual Health Exploration*. McKinsey Health Institute. https://www.mckinsey.com/mhi/our-insights/in-search-of-self-and-something-bigger-a-spiritual-health-exploration

[15] Peck, M. S. (1998). *People of the Lie: The Hope for Healing Human Evil*. Touchstone

[16] World Health Organization. (n.d.). *Coronavirus Disease (COVID-19) Pandemic*. https://www.who.int/europe/emergencies/situations/covid-19

[17] Fitzgerald, M., & Davis, E. Jr. (2022, Feb 25). *Russia Invades Ukraine: A Timeline of the Crisis*. U.S. News. https://www.usnews.com/news/best-countries/slideshows/a-timeline-of-the-russia-ukraine-conflict.

[18] B Lab. (n.d.). *About B Lab. B Lab is the Nonprofit Network Transforming the Global Economy to Benefit All People, Communities, and the Planet*. https://www.bcorporation.net/en-us/movement/about-b-lab/

Chapter 5

[19] Nightingale, E. (n.d.). *Earl Nightingale Quotes. Succeed Feed*. https://succeedfeed.com/earl-nightingale-quotes/

[20] Nightingale, E. (n.d.). *The Power of Integrity!* [Video]. YouTube. https://www.youtube.com/watch?v=2ELG6BGXDmM

[21] Covey, S. R. (2004). *The 7 Habits of Highly Effective People: Powerful Lessons in personal change* (Revised ed.). Free Press

[22] Maxwell, J. C. (2005). *Ethics 101: What Every Leader Needs to Know*. Center Street.

[23] Coelho, P. (2000). *The Devil and Miss Prym*. HarperCollins

[24] Casaubon, M. (Trans.). (n.d.). *The Meditations of Marcus Aurelius Antoninus*. Philaletheians. (Book 12 Section 13).

Chapter 6

[25] Wikipedia contributors. *I Still Believe* (Jeremy Camp song). Wikipedia, The Free Encyclopedia. https://en.wikipedia.org/wiki/I_Still_Believe_(Jeremy_Camp_song)

[26] Clear, J. (2018). *Atomic Habits: An Easy & Proven Way to Build Good Habits & Break Bad Ones*. Avery

Chapter 7

[27] Confucius. (n.d.). *Humility is the Solid Foundation of All Virtues*. BrainyQuote. https://www.brainyquote.com/quotes/confucius_141527

[28] Mother Teresa. (n.d.). *If You Are Humble Nothing Will Touch You, Neither Praise nor Disgrace, Because You Know What You Are.* Goodreads. https://www.goodreads.com/quotes/55677-if-you-are-humble-nothing-will-touch-you-neither-praise

[29] Emmons, R. A. (n.d.). Robert A. Emmons. *Gratitude Works*. University of California, Davis. https://emmons.faculty.ucdavis.edu/

Chapter 8

[30] Peale, N. V. (1952). *The Power of Positive Thinking*. Prentice-Hall Inc

[31] Hill, N. (1937). *Think and Grow Rich*. Napoleon Hill Foundation

[32] Byrne, R. (2006). *The Secret*. Atria Books/Beyond Words

[33] Robbins, T. (1992). *Awaken the Giant Within: How to Take Immediate Control of Your Mental, Emotional, Physical And Financial Destiny!*. Simon & Schuster

[34] Wikipedia contributors. (n.d.). *Serenity Prayer*. Wikipedia, The Free Encyclopedia. https://en.wikipedia.org/wiki/Serenity_Prayer

[35] Mayo Clinic Staff. (n.d.). *Stress Relief from Laughter? It's No Joke.* Mayo Clinic. https://www.mayoclinic.org/healthy-lifestyle/stress-management/in-depth/stress-relief/art-20044456

Chapter 9

[36] Sinek, S., Mead, D., & Docker, P. (2017). *Find Your Why: A Practical Guide for Discovering Purpose for You and Your Team*. Portfolio.

37 R. Polt, Trans.; T. Strong, Introduction (1997). Friedrich Nietzsche: *Twilight Of the Idols, or, How to Philosophize with the Hammer*. Hackett Publishing Company Inc. (Original work published 1889). (Section Epigrams and Arrows 12).

Chapter 10

38 Podolny, J. M., & Hansen, M. T. (2020, November–December). *How Apple is Organized for Innovation: It's About Experts Leading Experts*. Harvard Business Review. https://hbr.org/2020/11/how-apple-is-organized-for-innovation

39 Seth, S. (2024, April 14). *The BlackBerry Story: A Constant Cycle of Success and Failure*. Investopedia. https://www.investopedia.com/articles/investing/062315/blackberry-story-constant-success-failure.asp

40 Heikkilä, M., & Honan, M. (2024, October 31). *OpenAI Brings a New Web Search Tool to ChatGPT*. MIT Technology Review. https://www.technologyreview.com/2024/10/31/1106472/chatgpt-now-lets-you-search-the-internet/

41 Richardson, L. (2024, February 14). *How We're Partnering with the Industry, Governments and Civil Society to Advance AI*. Google Blog. https://blog.google/technology/ai/google-ai-partnerships-government-industry-civil-society/

42 O'Donnell, J. (2024, May 15). *OpenAI and Google are Launching Supercharged AI Assistants. Here's How You Can Try Them Out*. MIT Technology Review. https://www.technologyreview.com/2024/05/15/1092516/openai-and-google-are-launching-supercharged-ai-assistants-heres-how-you-can-try-them-out/

[43] Chowdhary, S., Kaushik, A., Soni, S., & Gupta, V. (2024, September 19). *Reimagining Healthcare Industry Service Operations in the Age of AI*. McKinsey & Company. https://www.mckinsey.com/industries/healthcare/our-insights/reimagining-healthcare-industry-service-operations-in-the-age-of-ai

[44] European Union. (n.d.). *Single Market: A Single Internal Market Without Borders.* https://european-union.europa.eu/priorities-and-actions/actions-topic/single-market_en

[45] ASEAN Secretariat. (2002). *Southeast Asia, A Free Trade Area.* ASEAN Secretariat

[46] Australia Department of Foreign Affairs and Trade. (n.d.*). Comprehensive and Progressive Agreement for Trans-Pacific Partnership.* https://www.dfat.gov.au/trade/agreements/in-force/cptpp/comprehensive-and-progressive-agreement-for-trans-pacific-partnership

[47] The Ministry of Commerce of the People's Republic of China. (n.d.). *China-ASEAN Free Trade Area.* http://fta.mofcom.gov.cn/topic/chinaasean

[48] Honey, S. (2024, February 13). *How the CPTPP Can Rewrite the Rules of 21st Century Trade*. Hinrich Foundation. https://www.hinrichfoundation.com/research/article/ftas/cptpp-rewrite-rules-of-21st-century-trade/

[49] European Parliament. (2024, January 25). *The EU's Digital Trade Policy (PE 757.615)*. European Union. https://www.europarl.europa.eu/thinktank/en/document/EPRS_BRI(2024)757615

50 United Nations Climate Change. (n.d.). *The Paris Agreement.*
UNFCCC. https://unfccc.int/process-and-meetings/the-paris-
agreement

51 Statista Research Department. (2024, April 11*). Impact of the Israel-
Hamas War on Shipping in the Red Sea.* Statista.
https://www.statista.com/topics/12046/impact-of-the-israel-hamas-
war-on-shipping-in-the-red-sea

52 Soni, P., & Coi, G. (2024, March 4). *By the Numbers*: *How Conflict in
the Red Sea Disrupts Global Trade.* Politico.
https://www.politico.eu/article/how-conflict-red-sea-disrupts-global-
trade-by-the-numbers-houthis-shipping/

53 Global Entrepreneur Institute. (n.d.). *Entrepreneurial Life Cycle.*
https://news.gcase.org/entrepreneurial-life-cycle/

54 Pădurean, L. (2023, February 5). *Nail it, Scale it, Sail it: An
Entrepreneurial Journey* [Video]. TEDxCluj. YouTube.
https://youtu.be/GmyXL3QbDLE

55 Wikipedia contributors. (n.d.). *gojek.* Wikipedia, The Free
Encyclopedia. https://en.wikipedia.org/wiki/Gojek

56 Tan, C. (2018, June 29). *CNBC Transcript: Nadiem Makarim,
founder and CEO, GO-JEK.* CNBC.
https://www.cnbc.com/2018/06/29/cnbctranscript-nadiem-makarim-
founder-and-ceo-go-jek.html

57 Acton Institute. (n.d.). *Lord Acton Quote Archive.* Acton Institute.
https://www.acton.org/research/lord-acton-quote-archive

58 De Smet, A., Gast, A., Lavoie, J., & Lurie, M. (2023, May 4*). New
Leadership for a New Era of Thriving Organizations.* McKinsey &
Company. https://www.mckinsey.com/capabilities/people-and-
organizational-performance/our-insights/new-leadership-for-a-new-
era-of-thriving-organizations

[59] Wikipedia contributors. (n.d.). *Ignorantia juris non excusat.* Wikipedia, The Free Encyclopedia. https://en.wikipedia.org/wiki/Ignorantia_juris_non_excusat

[60] Segal, T. (2024, June 3). *Enron Scandal and Accounting Fraud: What Happened?* Investopedia. https://www.investopedia.com/updates/enron-scandal-summary/

[61] Bondarenko, P. (2024, November 15). *Enron Scandal.* Encyclopaedia Britannica https://www.britannica.com/event/Enron-scandal/Downfall-and-bankruptcy

[62] Lioudis, N. (2024, October 7). *The Collapse of Lehman Brothers: A Case Study.* Investopedia. https://www.investopedia.com/articles/economics/09/lehman-brothers-collapse.asp

[63] Wikipedia contributors. (n. d). *Wirecard Scandal.* Wikipedia, The Free Encyclopedia. https://en.wikipedia.org/wiki/Wirecard_scandal

[64] Rubio, V. P. (2020, November 19). *Wirecard: Another FinTech Fraud.* Seven Pillars Institute for Global Finance and Ethics. https://mail.7pillarsinstitute.org/wirecard-another-fintech-fraud/

[65] Freeland, G. (2018, June 1). *Talent Wins Games, Teamwork Wins Championships.* Forbes. https://www.forbes.com/sites/grantfreeland/2018/06/01/talent-wins-games-teamwork-wins-championships/

[66] Whiting, K. (2023, July 12). *Here Are 11 of Nelson Mandela's Most Inspirational Quotes.* World Economic Forum. https://www.weforum.org/stories/2023/07/nelson-mandela-south-africa-quotes-madiba-inspiration/

[67] Washington University in St. Louis. (n.d.). *How Do You Define Leadership?* The Technology & Leadership Center. https://tlcenter.wustl.edu/the-career-confidant/defining-leadership

68 Wikipedia contributors. (n.d.). *Tuckman's Stages of Group Development*. Wikipedia, The Free Encyclopedia. https://en.wikipedia.org/wiki/Tuckman%27s_stages_of_group_development

69 Institute Success. (n.d.). *No One Cares How Much You Know Until They Know How Much You* Care - Theodore Roosevelt. https://institutesuccess.com/library/no-one-cares-how-much-you-know-until-they-know-how-much-you-care-theodore-roosevelt/

70 Neild, B. (2022, March 12). *The Incredible Story Behind Shackleton's Endurance Shipwreck*. CNN. https://edition.cnn.com/travel/article/story-behind-shackleton-endurance-shipwreck/index.html

Chapter 11

71 Mandela, N. (1994). *Long Walk to Freedom: The Autobiography of Nelson Mandela*. Little, Brown and Company

72 Plato. (2000). *Apology*. In G.M.A. Grube (Trans.), *Readings in Ancient Greek Philosophy: from Thales to Aristotle* (2nd ed., pp. 112-130). (Section 22d). Hackett Publishing Company

Chapter 12

73 Winfrey, O. (n.d.). *Passion Is Energy. Feel the Power That Comes from Focusing on What Excites You*. Pass It On. https://www.passiton.com/inspirational-quotes/7804-passion-is-energy-feel-the-poer-that-comes

74 Jobs, S. (2005). *Steve Jobs' Stanford University Commencement Speech*. CommonLit. (Page 3, Paragraph 15).

[75] Schwantes, M. (2020, April 24). *According to Jeff Bezos, This May Be the Best Definition of Success He's Ever Read.* Inc.com. https://www.inc.com/marcel-schwantes/according-to-jeff-bezos-this-may-be-best-definition-of-success-hes-ever-read.html

Chapter 13

[76] Kiyosaki, R. T. (1997). *Rich Dad Poor Dad: What the Rich Teach Their Kids About Money That the Poor and Middle Class Do Not!* Plata Publishing

[77] Miller, J. C. (2016). *Warren Buffett's Ground Rules: Words of Wisdom from the Partnership Letters of the World's Greatest Investor.* Harper Business

[78] Hagstrom, R. G. (2013). *The Warren Buffett Way.* John Wiley & Sons

Chapter 14

[79] Baker, R. (n.d.). *To Get Rich Never Risk Your Health. For it is The Truth that Health is the Wealth of Wealth.* BrainyQuote. https://www.brainyquote.com/quotes/richard_baker_176735

[80] Crichton-Stuart, C. (2023, January 12). *What Are the Benefits of Eating Healthy?* Medical News Today. https://www.medicalnewstoday.com/articles/322268

[81] Mayo Clinic Staff. (n.d.). *Exercise: 7 Benefits of Regular Physical Activity. Mayo Clinic.* https://www.mayoclinic.org/healthy-lifestyle/fitness/in-depth/exercise/art-20048389

[82] National Council on Aging. (2024, January 16). *10 Reasons Why Hydration is Important.* National Council on Aging. https://www.ncoa.org/article/10-reasons-why-hydration-is-important/

Chapter 15

[83] Felman, A., & Tee-Melegrito, R. A. (2024, March 22). *What is Mental Health?* Medical News Today. https://www.medicalnewstoday.com/articles/154543

[84] World Health Organization. (2022, June 17). *Mental Health*. World Health Organization. https://www.who.int/news-room/fact-sheets/detail/mental-health-strengthening-our-response

[85]Tolle, E. (1999). *The Power of Now: A Guide to Spiritual Enlightenment*. Namaste Publishing; New World Library.

[85] R. F. C. Hull, Trans (2014). *The Collected Work of C. G Jung. Volume 9 Part 1, The Archetypes and the Collective Unconscious*. Routledge and Princeton University Press. (Original work published 1934).

Chapter 16

[87] Wells, H. G. (n.d.). *Adapt or Perish, Now as Ever, is Nature's Inexorable Imperative*. BrainyQuote. https://www.brainyquote.com/quotes/h_g_wells_121062

Chapter 17

[88] Warren, R. (2013). *The Purpose Driven Life: What On Earth Am I Here For?* (10th Anniversary ed.). Zondervan.

[89] Coelho, P. (2006). *The Alchemist*. HarperTorch.

https://amytanbooks.com/

ALSO AVAILABLE

https://www.amazon.com/dp/B0DHL2Q6FX

Revisiting the Depths: Overcoming Fear and Finding Peace – A Journey of Transformation

ISBNs:

- eBook: 979-8-89283-133-8
- Paperback: 979-8-89283-134-5
- Hardcover: 979-8-89283-135-2
- Audiobook: 979-8-89283-172-7